God Speaks at Garabandal

The Message of Garabandal with a Summary and Picture Story of the Apparitions

by Joseph A. Pelletier, A.A.

1970
An Assumption Publication
500 Salisbury Street
Worcester, Massachusetts, 01609

Published with Ecclesiastical Approval

TO THOSE MANY FRIENDS whose
prayers, help in typing, editing and proof-
reading have contributed so much to this
book.

Contents

We exhort you to listen with simplicity of heart and honesty of mind to the salutary warnings of the Mother of God. The Roman pontiffs, . . . if they have been constituted the guardians and interpreters of the divine revelation contained in the Scriptures and in Tradition, also have the duty, when, after mature examination, they deem it necessary for the common good, of bringing to the attention of the faithful those supernatural lights which it pleases God to dispense freely to certain privileged souls, not for the purpose of presenting new doctrines, but rather to guide us in our conduct.

Pope John XXIII
Message for the closing of the Marian Year
February 18, 1959

Introduction

Apparitions are a dramatic means employed by a loving God to draw our attention to a message that he wishes to give us at a time of spiritual crisis. In this sense, as the goal that God has in mind, the message is always the most important thing. This book stresses the message. However, it also contains a summary and rather elaborate picture story of the apparitions.

The author is preparing another book, *Our Lady Comes to Garabandal,* which should appear in the late summer or fall of 1970. This will give a large place to the happenings of Garabandal, the *fantastic* happenings that include approximately two thousand apparitions and forty locutions, a "miracle of the visible Host," *llamadas* or calls, ecstatic marches, "kissed" objects, to mention but the more striking of the phenomena that was witnessed by many hundreds of thousands of people from 1961 to 1965.

The most unusual feature and the one that most strikingly distinguishes Garabandal from other well known apparitions, such as Lourdes and Fatima, is the ecstatic march. It is a phenomenon for which there is no natural explanation and which therefore points to the divine origin of the Garabandal event. It is also a unique instructional tool that is employed to reinforce Our Lady's verbal exhortations by dramatically demonstrating them in action. These concrete illustrations of the message, like the verbal messages themselves, all converge toward the correlative and embattled peaks of the Eucharist and the priesthood.

The urgent need at this time is for a systematic exposition of the message of Garabandal. This book attempts to fill that need.

HOW TO REACH GARABANDAL

It is a day's drive in a rented car from Madrid to Garabandal via Burgos, Corconte, Reinosa, Cabuerniga, Puentenansa and Cosio. An alternate route, longer but better, is via Burgos, Vargas, Torrelavega, Cabezon de la Sal, Cabuerniga, etc. Both routes are good. The road up the mountain from Cosio is undergoing major repairs.

You may also go from Madrid to Santander by plane (one a day on summer weekdays), train (several each day) or bus (a few a day). Santander (100,000 pop.) has only fair hotel accomodations with rooms quite scarce on summer weekends. Torrelavega, the next biggest city, has one second class hotel.

From Santander there is a train to Pesues. A bus leaves Pesues for Cosio at 10:00 A.M. and 8 P.M. A cab will take you from Pesues to Cosio for about $4.00. The special taxi from Cosio to Garabandal ($10.50) should be cheaper with the better road. You can rent a car at the Santander air port or from some city rental agencies. Terms are moderate. Taxis will take you from Santander to Cosio for $12.00.

There are no hotels close to Garabandal. Rooms in boarding houses or private homes are available on a limited scale in Puentenansa, Cosio or Garabandal. Rates are inexpensive as is the food.

Bilbao (300,000 pop.) has daily air flights from London and several weekly from Paris. It has good hotels and is slightly under 100 miles (about three hours by auto) from Santander.

1

The Apparitions
of Garabandal

The Village

Garabandal is a quaint hamlet of three hundred souls
isolated in the gorgeous Cantabrian mountains of
northwestern Spain. It lies about seventy miles south-
west of the provincial capital and episcopal see of
Santander. Some seventy solid rustic stone houses
stand huddled together on a narrow strip of land
overlooking the delightful wooded valley which
stretches southward toward the plain below.

Although perched high itself, San Sebastian de
Garabandal is surrounded on three sides and especially to the north by even loftier peaks of the same
picturesque mountain range. It is situated at the very
end of a winding and precarious four-mile cart road
cut into the mountain side that leads up from the
village of Cosio and the fertile valley below. A sol-
itary cluster of nine pines stands out starkly against
the horizon just above the town to the south.

The Pastor

It was the pastor of Cosio, Don Valentin Marichalar,
a simple and kindly man, who administered to the
spiritual needs of the souls of the isolated mountain

pueblo. He came up on horseback each Sunday to hear confessions and say Mass for the devout peasants in their own little church of Saint Sebastian. As soon as reports of the apparitions reached Cosio, he came up regularly, observed personally many of the ecstasies, questioned the four girls involved and took notes of what he saw and heard. He came to believe in the apparitions after proof was given to him by the vision in answer to a specific request he made.

Abstemious Life

The townfolk of Garabandal are a frugal lot. Their life is simple and hard. When the apparitions began in 1961 there was little electricity and no telephone at all in the village. Donkeys, cows, sheep, goats and chickens live in shelters underneath or beside the residents' humble homes. A stray donkey or cow can be seen day or night ambling unconcernedly through the streets. Straw from the little stables attached to the houses inevitably works itself into the streets adding to the dust and dirt of stony, unpaved surfaces.

An Angel Appears

The story of Garabandal opens on June 18, 1961, on a Sunday, at eight-thirty in the evening. Four simple, unsophisticated girls were playing in a sunken lane, called the *calleja,* at the southern extremity of the village. The sound of thunder was suddenly heard and later a brilliant angel appeared, first to Conchita (Maria Concepcion) Gonzalez, and then almost immediately afterward to Loli (Maria Dolores) Mazon, Jacinta Gonzalez and Maria Cruz Gonzalez. Notwithstanding the identical family names, none of the girls were closely related. The first three girls were twelve

years old and the fourth only eleven. However, because of the backward village environment, their
mental and psychological age was considerably less.
The angel came back eight more times in June.

A Mother and Her Children

The first time he spoke was on July 1st. He said:
"Do you know why I have come? It is to announce to
you that tomorrow, Sunday, the Virgin Mary will
appear to you as Our Lady of Mount Carmel." The
angel's mission was to prepare the children for Our
Lady's coming and to be her messenger. He returned
with her the next day but came back much less frequently after that. However, the Blessed Virgin began appearing almost every day and occasionally she
carried the Infant Jesus in her arms.

The four girls talked with the Blessed Virgin with
great simplicity. They talked about their everyday
life, about going out to the fields to make hay and
about getting bronzed by the sun. Our Lady delighted
in their childish talk.

A charming and almost disarming spontaneity
marked the apparitions. In her *Diary,* Conchita mentions that the angel and Our Lady smiled profusely
and that they laughed at some of their childish remarks. She says several times that the Blessed Virgin
kissed them. On a few occasions when she came
with the Infant Jesus, she allowed them to take him
in their arms. They also did simple little things to
amuse him, such as hiding pebbles in their sleeves
and in the tresses of their hair. Once, Our Lady took
the crown of small golden stars from her head and
allowed them to hold it in their hands. Many have
seen in all this an indication of the childlike attitude
we should have with Christ and his Blessed Mother.

Message Approved

Bishop Eugenio Beitia, one of the former bishops of Santander, issued a decree on July 8, 1965, in which he refused to recognize the supernatural character of the apparitions at Garabandal. However, in that same decree, he acknowledged the doctrinal integrity of the Garabandal message:

> We point out, however, that we have not found anything deserving of ecclesiastical censorship or condemnation either in the doctrine or in the spiritual recommendations that have been publicized as having been addressed to the faithful, for these contain an exhortation to prayer and sacrifice, to eucharistic devotion, to veneration of Our Lady in traditional praiseworthy ways, and to holy fear of God offended by our sins. They simply repeat the common doctrine of the Church in these matters.

Private Messages

Many of the messages delivered by Our Lady were of a purely private nature. Some were words of enlightenment or comfort directed to people who came to the village with personal problems. Others were statements that revealed the hidden thoughts or actions of people, several of whom were hesitant or doubting priests. Still others were predictions of future events, like that concerning "The Blind American," Joey Lomangino, which will be seen later.

Great Miracle Yet To Come

The Garabandal event is not yet over. Its climax will be a great miracle that shall convince everyone of the authenticity of Our Lady's visits to this remote Spanish mountain town. Conchita tells us about this in her *Diary* in the following words:

The Blessed Virgin advised me of a great miracle, saying that God, Our Lord, would perform it through her intercession. Just as the chastisement will be very, very great, in keeping with our deserts, so too, the miracle will be extremely great, in keeping with the needs of the world.

The Blessed Virgin has told me the date of the miracle and what it will consist of. I am supposed to announce it eight days in advance, so that people will come. The Pope will see it from wherever he is, and Padre Pio also. The sick who are present at the miracle will be cured and the sinners will be converted.

There will be no doubt in the mind of anyone who sees this great miracle which God, Our Lord, will perform through the intercession of the Blessed Virgin. And now as we await this great day of the miracle, let us see if the world changes and the chastisement is averted.

Padre Pio is reliably reported to have seen the miracle before he died. This should not astonish us, as we know that another person, Father Luis Andreu, S. J., also saw the miracle, as well as Our Lady, on August 8, 1961 six hours before he died. And Pope Pius XII saw the miracle of Fatima, the dancing sun, four times in the Vatican gardens thirty years after the original event took place in Portugal.

Conchita's manner of describing the greatness of the miracle is interesting. It "will be extremely great, in keeping with the needs of the world." Many feel that the world is in need of some great heavenly event to shake it up and bring it back to God. It should be noted that the chastisement is conditional. It can be averted "if the world changes."

Additional information concerning the miracle is given by Conchita in her report of a locution which she had with Our Lord on July 20, 1963. "Why is the miracle going to take place? To convert many people?", she asked Our Lord. "To convert the whole world," he answered. "Will Russia be converted?", she enquired. "Yes, she will be converted, and thus everyone—*todos*—will love our Hearts," he replied.

Conchita is the only one with whom the Blessed Virgin discussed the miracle. It will coincide with an event in the Church and with the feast of a saint who is a martyr of the Eucharist, and it will take place at eight-thirty on a Thursday evening. It will be visible not only to all those who are in the village but also to those in the surrounding mountains. It will be the greatest miracle that Jesus has performed for the world. There won't be the slightest doubt that it comes from God and that it is for the good of mankind. A sign of the miracle—*un señal del milagro,* which it will be possible to film or televise but not touch, will remain forever at the pines.

The Divine Warning

Conchita was advised by Our Lady at the pines on January 1, 1965 of a divine warning that would precede the great miracle. It will be seen and experienced by all men all over the world and will be a direct work of God. It will be very awesome. However, if men die from it, it will be only from the emotional shock of seeing it. It will take place before the miracle at a date unknown to Conchita and its purpose will be to give people a chance to amend their lives before that great heavenly sign. This topic will be elaborated upon in a later chapter.

Miracle of the Visible Host

A miracle to confirm the apparitions was requested

by the girls early in the apparitions. One was given to them, one that Conchita called a "little miracle", *un milagrucu,* using a diminutive proper to the Santander region. A visible host appeared suddenly and mysteriously on Conchita's tongue at one-forty in the morning on July 19, 1962. This precise miracle was announced fifteen days in advance by Conchita at the bidding of the archangel Saint Michael, who gave her the Communion. Many people were on hand for the event and one man, who was standing inches from Conchita, took some pictures of it.

Sufficient Proof Already Given

Other unusual things, for which there is no human explanation, also took place along with the apparitions or visions. These, particularly taken all together, constitute a powerful argument in favor of the authenticity of the event.

The three calls or *llamadas* which preceded and announced Our Lady's coming, the ecstatic marches, oscillations and falls, the children's excessive weight to others and exceptional lightness to each other in ecstasy, their humanly unexplainable knowledge of what people unknown to them had done or were thinking, and the kissing of objects by Our Lady and the amazing way they were distributed to people during the visions, these are some of the humanly unexplainable phenomena encountered at Garabandal.

Conchita Like Lucia of Fatima

Of the four girls involved in the events at Garabandal, Conchita is by far the most important. Her leading role can be compared to that of Lucia at Fatima. Not only is she, like Lucia, God's main agent among the visionaries, but she, too, has given us an historical document that will have to stand as the basic core of any account of the Garabandal happenings. Lucia wrote her *Memoirs* and Conchita has written her *Diary*. Both documents are simple and unpretentious. *Conchita's Diary* was started in 1962 when she was 13 and concluded in the last part of 1963 when she was still only 14. This spiritual journal has a directness and lack of sophistication that give it a real ring of authenticity, not to mention a very special charm.

There are other interesting points of similarity between Fatima and Garabandal in regard to the visionaries. In both cases there were several children involved, which assures the authenticity and accuracy of the message transmitted. Also, in each instance there is a difference in the degree to which each of the visionaries is involved in the event. At Fatima, Lucia did all the speaking to the vision and Francisco never heard the Lady's voice. At Garabandal, Conchita saw Our Lady over a longer period of time than the other girls and she was the one who had the most *locutions,* which are something peculiar to this Spanish event as compared to Lourdes and Fatima.

Loli is next in importance and she enjoys considerable more prominence than either Jacinta or Maria Cruz. We really know very little of Jacinta, who is reticent by nature, and even less of Maria Cruz.

Mission of Suffering

In the early days of the apparitions, Our Lady foretold that there would come a time of denials and contradictions on the part of the visionaries and their parents. These predictions have been fulfilled and have brought great moral suffering to all concerned and particularly to Conchita. Our Lady and Our

Lord had told Conchita that she would have much to suffer for the world as part of her mission in life.

Garabandal Unique Event

Garabandal is unique in the history of Marian apparitions and this for a number of reasons. The number of apparitions, somewhere in the vicinity of two thousand, is amazing. The appearance and extensive use of a new means of heavenly communication not usually encountered along with apparitions having a public message, namely, the locution, sets it apart from Lourdes and Fatima. The span of time over which the apparitions (June 18, 1961 to November 13, 1965) and locutions (about April 1963 to February, 1966) occurred, is exceptional. The things announced for the future and yet to come—the warning, the great miracle and the permanent sign at the pines, and the conditional chastisement, are most unusual. The variety of the sites where the visions took place—in the church, at the door of the church, in homes, on various streets of the village, at the pines, in the cemetery—, is astonishing. The time at which they took place, literally at every hour of the day and night, is quite uncommon. The abundance of secondary or supporting mystical phenomena, such as the miracle of the visible Host, the *llamadas* or calls and the ecstatic marches and falls, is almost overwhelming. The trials of the visionaries, the difficulties and opposition that have accompanied the events almost continually are so unusual that there does not seem to be any natural explanation for them. The manner in which Garabandal has overcome all obstacles and become more and more widely known and accepted, is another of its astounding facets.

2

Picture Story of the Garabandal Event

Garabandal, village on a mountain surrounded by mountains.
Road from Cosio is cut into slope at right. Cluster of pines over-
looks the pueblo from the south.

Eastern and central part of Garabandal as one enters from north by road from Cosio which ends in the village. 70 closely huddled homes and 300 people make up the pueblo. St. Michael's chapel, requested by Our Lady, in center between village and pines.

Girls at beginning of apparitions. L. to r. Loli, Jacinta, Maria Cruz and Conchita. Conchita's pigtails were cut at end of July, 1961, at Santander where she was called for questioning by diocesan authorities. House at upper left was Loli's home at time of apparitions and scene of a number of visions. House at right her present home.

Cross marks spot in *calleja* where all early apparitions, both of angel and of Our Lady, took place (June 18 through July, 1961). Some later ones occurred here, too. Blessed Virgin ordered girls to come here and say rosary, occasionally at 5 or 6 a.m. in winter. Penance was important part of Garabandal message.

The *cuadro* or corral erected in *calleja* at spot of early apparitions to protect the girls from spectators. Guardia Civil came from valley below. Note steep incline and loose stones. Girls in ecstasy came down here backward in dark at high speed and never slipped or fell.

Last steep slope from end of the *calleja* to the pines, the most incredible part of the backward estatic marches. Girls' eyes were always raised above.

The pines, planted by Conchita's grandfather. Our Lady appeared before all nine. Many visions occurred here, such as the one involving the four girls and during which Fr. Luis Andreu, S.J., saw Our Lady and the miracle (girls never saw the miracle). Final apparation, Nov. 13, 1965, which centered on kissed objects, also took place here.

Jacinta and Loli in forward ecstatic march. Girls were never fatigued by rapid ecstatic marches or by visions of several hours duration.

Jacinta and Loli in backward ecstatic march. Jacinta's raised leg and bent knees of girls at left would indicate quick pace. Note how Loli is avoiding protruding stone.

Successive phases of ecstatic march, Sept. 11, 1961, at 5 p.m. Loli, looking at vision, leaves Conchita's house followed by her father Ceferino. He accompanied her often. Seconds later, tempo of march increases.

Loli, only one in ecstasy, holds Conchita's left hand, Maria Cruz's right hand. Jacinta holds Maria Cruz's hand. Loli is in full ecstatic flight around corner of Conchita's house. Extended arms, inclined torso and sharply raised left leg indicate acceleration of her pace. Some marches were so fast spectators could hardly keep up with girls.

Vision in the *quadro* (note fence pole) of the *calleja* in summer of 1961. All four girls were involved in early days of apparitions. Girls all hold a rosary which was recited during every apparition. Our Lady requested daily recitation of rosary. Pulse of two end girls is being taken. L. to r. Loli, Conchita, Jacinta and Maria Cruz.

Mood and expression of all four girls changed frequently and simultaneously, reflecting various degrees of seriousness, sadness and joy. This rules out possibility of hallucination, according to Dr. R. Puncernau, eminent neurologist from Barcelon, who examined girls several times in and out of estasy. He also holds that there is no natural explanation for all the phenomena taken together.

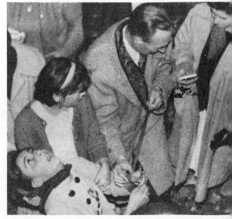

Dr. Celestino Ortiz, pediatrician from Santander, shown taking the pulse of Conchita in ecstasy. He spent some 50 days, at intervals, examining the girls. He, like Dr. Puncernau, maintain that the girls were healthy and normal in every way.

Loli, Conchita, Jacinta and Maria Cruz in ecstasy, holding rosaries and medals given to them by the people for kissing by Our Lady. She said her Son would perform "prodigies" through these objects she had kissed. Great bodily and spiritual graces have been received through them all over the world.

Reaching for Our Lady's kiss (same vision). A priest looks on. Some one thousand priests saw the girls in ecstasy. Many believed. Conchita's mother is at lower left. She attended most ecstacies.

Conchita receiving invisible but real Communion from St. Michael. Girls were prepared by angel for some time prior to first real Communion, and were taught to make adequate thanksgiving. Angel said he took Hosts from "tabernacles of the earth."

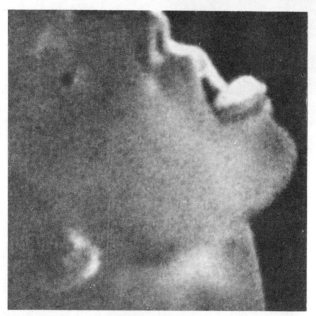

Photo of "the miracle of the visible Host." Picture taken by amateur with only pocket flashlight illumination. Conchita extended tongue and Host suddenly appeared, remaining visible for some two minutes. At Our Lady's request, miracle was announced 15 days in advance and large gathering was on hand. Close bystanders assured there was no fraud.

Church of San Sebastian, focal point of apparitions. Visions sometimes began in church or under porch. Girls in ecstasy often entered church and prayed before Blessed Sacrament until this was banned by diocesan authorities. After ban, they walked in ecstasy around church, saying rosary and singing Hail Holy Queen, and they prayed at door. After each vision, girls generally went to church for "station" to Blessed Sacrament. Locutions (began, spring of 1963) often occurred in church. St. Michael brought girls Communion occasionally under church porch when it was not available otherwise.

Four girls, arm-in-arm in ecstasy, crossed narrow bridge in foreground: two end girls walked "on air."

At door of church, one visionary easily lifts other "to reach Our Lady." Girls in ecstasy were practically weightless to each other, but excessively heavy to others who tried to lift them.

Jacinta and Maria Cruz answering "third" call or *llamada*. Conchita says in *Diary* that they were "carried by the Blessed Virgin" to place of apparition. There was no exertion or fatigue, though they ran. Three spaced calls preceded Our Lady's first visit on a given day. Calls were interior summons without words, feeling of joy and expectancy, each stronger than preceding. Interval between calls varied but was progressively shorter from 1st to 3rd. Vision followed 3rd call in matter of minutes.

Ecstasy of June 18, 1965. Conchita receives Our Lady's 2nd message from St. Michael. Announced more than six months in advance, a great gathering (140 foreign cars, over 30 photographers and movie-camera men, the Italian Television) was on hand. Our Lady complained 1st message had not been heeded and "cup was flowing over."

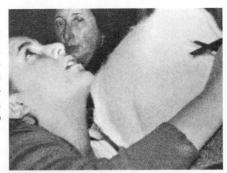

Loli places kissed medal and chain around neck without looking. Girls in ecstasy returned kissed objects to rightful owners, even when completely unknown to them.

Gonzalez family, Aug. 1969: Miguel, Conchita, Joey Lomangino, who is like a brother, Aniceta, the mother, and Serafin.

Maria Cruz and her home, July, 1968.

Loli with baby brother and mother Julia, July, 1968.

3

What about Garabandal?

Views of Doctors and Theologians

In the summer of 1962, a Spanish theologian prepared some notes on Garabandal for Doctor Ricardo
Puncernau, a neurologist and Assistant Professor at
the Medical School of Barcelona. (The theologian's
name is withheld because of the private nature of
the document.) Here are some of the more pertinent
observations made by this theologian:

> A study of the information given by the doctors
> (Dr. Ortiz of Santander, a children's specialist, spent
> 22 consecutive days studying the little girls) convinces
> me that any normal or abnormal psychological ex-
> planation is unthinkable.
>
> [Author's note: Doctor Puncernau is himself one
> of the top medical authorities on Garabandal. He saw
> the girls in ecstasy some twenty times and examined
> them very thoroughly both in and out of ecstasy. He
> concurs that there is no natural (either normal or
> pathological) explanation for the happenings of
> Garabandal.]
>
> The rules suggested to us by the great masters of
> the spiritual life for the discernment ⸱⸱ spirits ⸱ ⸱ ⸳s us
> no indication, in the case of San Sebastian de Gara-
> bandal, of possible diabolical possession. There is no
> trace of worldly spirit, vainglory, desire for money,
> or pride.

Numbers of religious men, wise, prudent and virtuous, who have visited San Sebastian de Garabandal, are inclined towards a supernatural interpretation. Among them are some of the outstanding theologians that we have in Spain today. . . .

I believe that there is a serious and more than sufficient foundation for belief in the reality of the apparitions of the Blessed Virgin Mary to the four little girls at San Sebastian of Garabandal.

Attitude of the Church

There have been several statements from the various bishops of Santander since the start of the apparitions —all have refused to admit the divine origin of the events at Garabandal. Although Rome has steadfastly left the matter of the apparitions in the hands of the local bishops, it has nevertheless shown a personal interest in them.

Conchita was called to Rome by Cardinal Ottaviani and went there in January of 1966. She visited the Holy Office and spent two-and-a-half hours there in a very cordial interview. A few days after this visit she participated in a public audience. The Holy Father paused before Conchita and said: "I bless you, and with me, the whole Church blesses you." This cannot be interpreted as approval of Garabandal, but it is not without significance.

Also, there have been a number of private statements relative to Garabandal that have emanated from high places in the eternal city. Although none of them would warrant saying that Rome has approved the apparitions, they do indicate that Church authorities there are much more open to Garabandal than Santander has been up to now, and that the Holy See does not consider the matter closed because of statements that have been issued by Santander.

Apparitions Still Under Investigation

Finally, there is definitely an open-mindedness in Rome that has not been found in the past at Santander. And from all appearances, it is an open-mindedness that does not rule out the possibility of eventual acceptance and approval of the events at Garabandal. All this is well summed up in a reply given in 1969 by Cardinal Seper, head of the Doctrinal Congregation, when he was asked by an American woman if she could legitimately speak about Garabandal in the United States. He said that she could as long as she made it clear that the matter was under investigation.

A formal approval of the Garabandal event, either by Santander or Rome, would not appear likely until we have had the great miracle, which precisely was promised by heaven to authenticate irrefutably this most unusual and fascinating series of happenings that God has provided for his Church in crisis.

The happenings of Garabandal are still under investigation and the author does not presume to anticipate the final judgment of the Church. He feels that writing about these events is fully in keeping with the present mind of the Church as expressed in the documents of Vatican II and further emphasized by the Holy See's suppression in 1966 of the old restrictive rules concerning the writing and publication of books and pamphlets on reported apparitions. This recent abrogation of the entire Index of Forbidden Books section of Canon Law means that the Church no longer requires the Imprimatur for writing on new apparitions which are still under investigation. The author has simply wanted to make known an event that would seem to be of considerable importance but wishes to remind the reader that only the Church can speak the final word on Garabandal.

The Final Word Rests with Rome

There are two questions that cause much confusion in many minds in regard to apparitions like those of Garabandal, namely, what is the supreme Church authority in such matters and what is the value of an approval when it is finally granted. A statement made by Cardinal Patriarch Cerejeira of Lisbon at the closing of the Jubilee Year of Fatima, in October, 1942, will help to clarify both of these points. Referring to the approval of the Fatima visions granted by the Bishop of Fatima (Leiria) on October 13, 1930 (13 years after the final apparition!) he stated:

> This approbation is not irrefutable and the Holy See can either confirm or annul it. Even though it is confirmed by the Holy See, it does not possess the force or value of a definition of faith, since the facts of the apparitions of Fatima belong to the body of proved historical truths, not to the deposit of faith.

4

Are Apparitions Relevant to Our Times?

In this age when everything is being examined with a critical eye, one has to ask the question: "Are apparitions, such as those of Lourdes and Fatima, a thing of the past or do they have a place in the Church today?" Are they relevant to our times? What is their meaning?

There is a vital bond between the divine manifestations of the Old Testament, the miracles of Christ, and the visitations of Mary that we call apparitions. To perceive this link of continuity is to see apparitions in their proper perspective. They then take on their true and sacred meaning as manifestations of God's continually renewed action and intervention for his People. However, the incarnation of the divine or supernatural in a historical fact is always mysterious and disconcerting. It takes humility and faith to accept it.

In Marian apparitions, the past takes on new life and becomes present again. It is Cana all over again. Christ at the word of his Mother, healing the sick, giving the grace of repentance to sinners, leading the good to greater spiritual heights.

It is also the more remote past coming to life

again. It is a reliving of the days of God's first marvels for his Chosen People, the prodigies performed in Old Testament times. It is a manifestation of that same power and fidelity that God showed when he led his people through the Red Sea, into the promised land, when he gave them victory at Jericho, brought them back from exile and provided them with the means of rebuilding the Temple. It is another instance of the *mirabilia Dei* of saving history. To use the words of Mary, which she herself borrowed from the Old Testament, it is "He who is mighty doing great things for his People, showing might with his arm, giving help to his People, mindful of his mercy."

In modern Marian apparitions we find the same fundamental characteristic that marked both the marvels of old and those performed by Christ. They all involve a personal intervention of God and it is this that gives them their sacred significance, their religious meaning.

The great hidden God, the mysterious God who is so patient and slow to act that he seems deaf or indifferent, suddenly comes alive at a particular place and time in history. He appears, he talks, he performs wondrous deeds. The means he takes does not matter. It may be the wind, a cloud, a column of fire, bread from heaven, water from a stone, a prophet, an angel, or Mary, the mother of God. But it is always he, who through these things and persons, shows himself to us and talks to us.

It is God through these various intermediaries establishing a personal relationship with each and every one of us. The invisible, apparently dead God, has shown himself to me. He has brought me a message. He has loved me.

Of course, God was never deaf nor dead. He has always loved me, spoken to me and done things for me, even though his love, his words and his deeds, have not always been that apparent. But through these marvels he has brought himself down to my human level. He has become visibly embodied in these various manifestations, old and new. I have seen him with my eyes, heard him with my ears, and identified him experientially.

In modern Marian apparitions I recognize the same God of love who healed and forgave in the Old Testament, who healed and forgave through his incarnate Son. These modern marvels of his, like those of old, are miracles of deliverance, liberation, both physical and spiritual. And as always, the small and the humble are the first to recognize him in the ways that he chooses to come to us.

The Basic Purpose Always the Same

Another important feature that unites God's old and new manifestations is the sameness of their ultimate purpose, a reform of heart. They all involve a call to conversion. The call God made through Isaiah: "Turn to me and be saved" (45:22), and that was echoed all through the Old Testament, was repeated by John the Baptist (Mt 3:2), and finally by Christ Himself (Mk 1:15). It is also the fundamental theme that underlies the messages of Lourdes, Fatima and Garabandal, and that is why all these messages have such an authentic ring to them. They are all a pressing invitation to a change of heart, to a personal spiritual renewal. "People must not offend God any more, for he is already greatly offended," were Our Lady's parting words at Fatima and those which Lucia says impressed her most of all. "Above all, we must lead good lives," or to translate literally, "we must be good—*tenemos que ser buenos*," was the basic recommendation at Garabandal.

All the other parts of these Marian messages, such as praying and doing penance, marching in processions, visiting the Blessed Sacrament, are means for obtaining the grace that will help us purify our hearts and live holy lives.

Visions Nothing New

The very vehicle of God's modern manifestations to us have an antecedent in sacred history. Visions and apparitions are indeed nothing new in the history of the People of God. In the Old Testament, God at various times sent angels to deliver his messages to men. He sent an angel to Abraham by the oaks of Mamre and to Moses in the burning bush, etc. At the time of the coming of Christ, he sent an angel to Zacharias in the temple, then the archangel Gabriel to Mary, the virgin of Nazareth, and finally, an angel in dreams to Joseph, Mary's spouse. After the birth of Christ, angels were sent by God to the Apostles Peter and Paul to help them in their work for the Church. And now in our own days, God continues to send angels with his messages. He sent them at Fatima and at Garabandal. But the principal bearer of his messages in recent times is Mary, the Mother of the Redeemer. God is free to speak to us through whom he wills. The important thing for us to consider is not so much who carries the message, but who sent the message.

Divine Directives at Times of Spiritual Crisis

To appreciate fully the message God gives the world through apparitions such as those of Lourdes, Fatima and Garabandal, it is important to be well acquainted with the condition of the Church at the precise moment of history in which the message is imparted. For much of the significance of apparitions derives from the fact that they are divine commands telling us what to do at a particular moment in the history of the Church, usually a moment of spiritual crisis. They are not doctrinal revelations and they add nothing to the deposit of the faith which ended with the death of the last apostle. They are clear and precise directives (instruction, warning, exhortation to penance, recommendation of a particular devotion, etc.), usually expressed in very simple terms, that are given by a benign God to guide the actions of his People in some period of spiritual need.[1]

Apparitions Part of Charismatic Element of Church

Karl Rahner points out that man is moved much more readily and effectively by the divine intervention that we call apparitions than by an abstract message or statement of principle from astute theologians or the hierarchy of the Church. And God who knows man's heart and mind takes him as he is and has recourse to the means that are most productive. He speaks to him in times of crisis, when there is urgent need that he listen and respond, through the impressive and effective charismatic instrumentality of an apparition. It would seem that God speaks to us through apparitions when other means have failed. But it should be remembered that charismatic intervention or activity is a normal concomitant of the possession of the Holy Spirit and therefore a permanent gift in the Church. Apparitions are part of the

[1] See St. Thomas Aquinas, *Summa,* 2a 2ae, q. 174, art. 6, ad 3um; Karl Rahner, *Visions and Prophecies,* pp. 108-109.

charismatic element of the Church and as such represent a vital stirring of the Spirit for the growth and welfare of the People of God.

The messages, then, given by God through such apparitions as Lourdes, Fatima and Garabandal, are commands or directives given by God to his People and indicating the things they should do, the religious or devotional practices they need to adopt or maintain at some precise historical time of spiritual need. Even the prophetic elements contained in such messages are directly related to action and attitudes and have as their immediate purpose to inspire and direct the People of God.

Message of Garabandal—Preventive Antidote

Seen in the light of these considerations, the message of Garabandal is particularly significant. It appears as a preventive antidote prepared for the faithful by a loving God in view of an important spiritual tempest about to break upon the Church. The apparitions started in the summer of 1961 whereas the storm over the Church only began to gather with the opening of the Ecumenical Council Vatican II in the fall of 1962. The storm developed and broke during the Council and has been increasing in fury ever since.

At Garabandal, God anticipated the trouble and gave us the remedy for it before it occurred. Mary, the rosary, the scapular and sacramentals, penance, reflection on the passion of Christ and on heaven and hell, sorrow for sins and conversion of life, visiting the Blessed Sacrament in our churches, prayer for priests, bishops, and cardinals on the verge of eternal damnation, respect for the authority of the Church, the existence of angels and modesty, these are all parts of the Garabandal message and things that have come under attack in our day. Through the apparitions at Garabandal, God prepared us ahead of time for the tempest that would rock the boat of the Church. He knew that it would break with such fury that it would strike fear in the hearts of many. So he threw out the anchor to us in advance of its coming.

Messages have Dogmatic Connotation

The messages of such apparitions do not include new doctrinal revelations. They add nothing to the deposit of faith. Yet, they are not completely disso-ciated from dogma and the deposit of faith which they often serve to illustrate or confirm.

At Lourdes in 1858, God confirmed the dogma of the Immaculate Conception proclaimed four years earlier by Pius IX. Some had been upset by the definition of this dogma whose scriptural roots were difficult to trace and Lourdes was seen as a heavenly seal of approval on what the Pope had done. Berna-dette herself had noted this and pointed it out in a letter sent to the Pope in 1867.

At Garabandal there are quite evident dogmatic or doctrinal connotations in regard to a number of the parts of the message. Garabandal, like all Marian apparitions, is a confirmation of the Church's tradi-tional teaching concerning Mary's power of interces-sion and her active role in our salvation. There are also obvious doctrinal overtones in the Garabandal message in regard to the priesthood, the Eucharist and other topics, as will be seen later.

5

The Various Messages
of Garabandal

God's Messengers

Our Lady came to Garabandal, as she came to
Lourdes and Fatima, as God's messenger. Although
it was she who spoke to the four girls, Conchita, Loli,
Jacinta and Maria Cruz, it was God's voice or message that we heard, whence the title of this book.
By the same token, the girls of Garabandal were in
the final analysis, God's messengers.

Simple People

One of the means that God uses to authenticate his
message is the choice he makes of his earthly messengers, simple untutored people, usually children.
Catherine Labouré, God's human intermediary for
the Miraculous Medal, with the humility and truthful-
ness so characteristic of the saints, expressed this
well in terms that apply basically not only to her, but
also to Bernadette, the three little shepherds of Fatima and the four girls of Garabandal: "I did not
know anything, not even how to write. It is in the
religious community that I learned what I know and

41

that is why the Blessed Virgin chose me, so that people would not be able to doubt."[1]

The Messages of Garabandal

It is very deceptive to speak of the message of Garabandal in the singular. There were two formal messages, messages given specifically as such. The first message was given to the four girls by Our Lady herself on July 4, 1961, and announced publicly at her request on October 18 of that year. The second message was delivered to Conchita alone in Our Lady's name by the archangel Saint Michael on June 18, 1965.

Also, the entire Garabandal event comprised some two thousand apparitions and some forty or more locutions. Messages of varying kinds and importance were imparted on all these occasions. These might be called informal messages, but they were frequently important and very definitely form part of the total Garabandal message. For example, nothing was said of the rosary in either of the two so-called "messages" of 1961 and 1965. Yet Our Lady spoke of the rosary every time she appeared and she made specific requests concerning it. All this was surely meant for the whole world and not only for the girls.

God Speaks through Persons, Places and Events

In addition to these spoken messages, formal and informal, there were the messages which were conveyed through the persons, places and events involved in the various happenings that form part of the entire Garabandal story. The presence of an angel, the prom-

---

[1] Edmon Crapez, *La Vénérable Cathérine Labouré* (Paris: J. Gabalda, 1910), p. 186. The translation is the author's.

inent place given to Holy Communion, these and other facts have a meaning and a message for us.

One of the intriguing things about the Garabandal event is its many facets. This means that its message is not simple. Even the two official messages of 1961 and 1965, though very simple in their wording, are not as simple as they might seem. There is much more depth to them than appears on the surface and there is also an intimate relationship between the various parts of these messages which is not immediately obvious.

The Message of October 18, 1961

We must make many sacrifices, perform much penance, and visit the Blessed Sacrament frequently.

But first, we must lead good lives.

If we do not, a chastisement will befall us.

The cup is already filling up and if we do not change, a very great chastisement will come upon us.[1]

The Message of June 18, 1965

As my message of October 18 [1961] has not been complied with and has not been made known to the

[1] There exist two slightly different texts of this 1961 message. The first was written by Conchita and signed by her and the other three girls. The second is found in *Conchita's Diary*. As the first text was written about a year before the second and was signed by all four girls, it has been preferred here. The difference between the two texts involves two words. In the *Diary* text, "frequently" is omitted in the statement: "We must . . . visit the Blessed Sacrament." And "very" is added in the statement: "We must lead very good lives-*Tenemos que ser muy buenos* (literally: we must be very good)." It might also be noted that the first text ends with this remark: "The Blessed Virgin wants us to do these things, so that we may avoid God's punishment."

world, I am advising you that this is the last one.

Before, the cup was filling up. Now it is flowing over.

Many cardinals, many bishops and many priests[2] are on the road to perdition and are taking many souls with them.

Less and less importance is being given to the Eucharist.

You should turn the wrath of God away from yourselves by your efforts.

If you ask his forgiveness with sincere hearts, he will pardon you.

I, your Mother, through the intercession of Saint Michael the archangel, ask you to amend your lives.

You are now receiving the last warnings.

I love you very much and do not want your condemnation.

Pray to us with sincerity and we will grant your requests.

You should make more sacrifices. Think about the passion of Jesus.

[2] Many books carry a different and shorter text: "Many priests are on the road. . . ." These are not the exact words transmitted to Conchita during the apparition. Father Marcelino Andreu, S.J., brother of the famous Father Luis Andreu, S.J., stood at Conchita's left side during the June 18, 1965 apparition. He is now a missionary in Taiwan. In his Mission Letter #3 for his friends in the United States and Canada dated October 18, 1969, he states: "The message that was released to the public by Conchita was the third copy she wrote, which differs a little from the first two copies of the original message she wrote, which, given by Saint Michael, reads as follows: 'Many cardinals, many bishops and many priests are . . . .' When Conchita was asked why she dropped 'cardinals and bishops,' her explanation was that cardinals and bishops are priests." Conchita has spoken of this matter many times and has insisted that she omitted the words on her own initiative and not because of pressure from others.

6

The Renewal of Private Prayer and the Rosary

The Private Prayer and Rosary Messages of Lourdes, Fatima and Garabandal

So much for the general background information needed to understand and appreciate the charismatic significance of the apparitions and message of Garabandal. What now is the prayer message and more particularly the rosary message given to us by the Blessed Virgin at that Spanish mountain village?

The message of the rosary as taught at Garabandal cannot be fully understood unless it is examined in its proper perspective, that is, unless it is viewed against the backdrop of the rosary messages of Lourdes and Fatima. For there is a clear thread of continuity concerning the rosary (and other things as well) that runs through all three of these great modern apparitions.

One of the first things that strikes anyone who studies Lourdes, Fatima and Garabandal is the strong emphasis placed by Our Lady on the rosary at all three places. It is the only specific prayer recommended at each of the three places by the Blessed Virgin herself. And it is interesting to note that there is a certain gradation in the way it is presented to us at each site.

At Lourdes, the recommendation of the rosary was completely silent though most eloquent. Our Lady carried the rosary on her arm. That in itself is quite significant. Yet something else occurred at Lourdes that is at least equally expressive. The two initial apparitions and four of the others including the final and eighteenth one, were taken up solely with the recitation of the rosary by Bernadette. Our Blessed Mother did not speak to the child and was content to watch in silence as she prayed. She herself simply counted the beads as Bernadette said Hail Mary after Hail Mary. That the Blessed Virgin should appear *six times* to a little girl for no other reason than to watch her recite the rosary is something certainly unique and not without meaning in regard to the rosary. It should be added that during the greater part of the other twelve Lourdes apparitions, when Bernadette was not actually speaking with her heavenly visitor, she spent the time reciting the rosary while Our Lady followed silently on her own beads.

At Fatima, Our Lady asked for the recitation of the rosary explicitly. It is as though she felt we had missed the point of her silent recommendation at Lourdes, and she wanted to make sure this time that we would really get her message, or, more precisely, the message of the Almighty who sent her. And she took no chance of our not understanding. She asked the children to say the rosary at each and every one of her six apparitions. And according to Sister Lucia's *Memoirs,* at five of these six appearances she asked them to say it "every day."

The Blessed Virgin stated twice at Fatima that she wanted a little chapel built in honor of Our Lady of the Rosary. Indeed, that is the name she finally used to identify herself on the occasion of the last apparition which took place during October, the month of the rosary. Finally, she taught the children a prayer to be said after each decade of the rosary: "O My Jesus, forgive us; save us from the fires of hell; lead all souls to heaven, especially those in greatest need [that is, in greatest danger of damnation]."

The little shepherds of Fatima took Our Lady's message to heart and put the rosary into their daily lives. The three of them would say the rosary together in the morning before leaving home for pasture with their sheep and again on returning with them at the end of the afternoon. They would also recite it together once or twice during the day while out with the sheep. And little Francisco, whom Our Lady said would go to heaven on condition that he say many rosaries, used to recite another five decades alone by himself three or four times each day, for a total of seven or eight rosaries every day!

Now at Garabandal, Our Lady went even further regarding the rosary and actually taught the four girls how to say the rosary properly. And she taught them in a very detailed and concrete manner, as shall be seen.

Why Garabandal?

A formal message of Garabandal was given twice, once on October 18, 1961 and later in a longer and more complete form on June 18, 1965. But neither form of the message makes any mention of the rosary.

If the rosary was not explicitly mentioned in the formal message of Garabandal, it was most clearly and powerfully taught to us on innumerable occasions through the approximately two thousand apparitions that make up the main part of the Garabandal event. And it was even taught to us at Garabandal before the apparitions started.

A question that comes to mind quite naturally when one is considering an apparition or series of apparitions is: why did God choose this particular locality? One can legitimately look for something in the religious history of the immediate area where an apparition occurs that will tie in with the heavenly message delivered there. At Fatima, where Our Lady stressed the rosary in such explicit terms, one is not at all surprised to discover that prior to 1917 there had been in that region a strong tradition of faithfulness to this form of prayer. And one suspects that there is some connection between this tradition of the rosary in the Fatima area and the great Dominican monastery of Batalha only twenty-five miles away, where once upwards of a hundred sons of Saint Dominic prayed and preached the rosary.

The author knew of these facts concerning the rosary tradition in the Fatima region and he wondered whether something similar might not also be true at Garabandal. He received his answer at Garabandal itself and in a rather dramatic way. He was walking along through the pitch dark streets of the village at nine o'clock at night on a Monday, his very first at the pueblo. He heard the church bells ring and could not imagine why this was happening at such a late hour on a weekday night. Then, a few days later, on the feast of Saint James or Santiago de Compostela, which is a national holiday in Spain, he was talking with Conchita at three o'clock in the afternoon when the same church bells rang out again. When questioned about them, she told him that the bells were tolling to invite the people to the recitation of the rosary in the village church. Later he discovered that the church bells ring in the pueblo for the common recitation of the rosary every single day of the week and that this has been going on for years and longer than anyone can remember. The hour of the recitation varies with the seasons and the days. If the priest is not there on a particular day, some woman or child leads the people in prayer. So Garabandal, too, has a religious history that links it closely with the message of the rosary.

Why These Children?

Another question that comes even more naturally to mind in investigating an apparition is: why did God choose the particular people who were favored with the vision? Did they possess specific qualities or virtues that made them especially worthy instruments of God in this particular case? Is there some connection between their lives and the message God imparted at this special place? If we examine Lourdes, Fatima and Garabandal we find that at all three places the visionaries gave definite proof of their personal attachment to the rosary. In each instance we find that the children spontaneously prayed the rosary while waiting for an apparition to take place. This they definitely did on their own, without anyone telling them to do so. They prayed it through personal conviction and they prayed it with faith in its efficacy, trusting that through the rosary they would attract or hasten the coming of their heavenly visitor.

The Specific Rosary Message of Garabandal

At Lourdes and also at Fatima Our Lady appeared with the rosary hanging visibly from her hand or arm. At Garabandal it was the scapular rather than the rosary that hung from her arm. But at Garabandal Our Lady instructed the girls on how to say the rosary in a new way. We touch here the key feature of the Garabandal rosary message, the new element that adds something important to the rosary message of both Lourdes and Fatima. Our Lady actually taught Conchita, Loli, Jacinta and Maria Cruz how to recite it in a manner that is simple yet different than anything to which we are accustomed.

We have here not only the most important element of the Garabandal rosary message as compared to that of Lourdes and Fatima, but also one of the most vital parts of the entire Garabandal message. The significance of this particular factor, the proper praying of the rosary, derives from the importance of prayer itself, the absolutely essential matter of prayer, which, from the human point of view, can be said to be the starting point of all spiritual good. And it does not matter that we are dealing here with private or individual prayer and not with liturgical or public prayer. Private prayer is important in its own right and as such is strongly recommended in the *Constitution on the Liturgy*.[1] Unfortunately, it has been seriously neglected in the great stress on liturgical prayer.

Applies to All Private or Vocal Prayer

At Garabandal, Our Lady was concerned with the renewal of all private or vocal prayer and not just with the renewal of the rosary. According to *Conchita's Diary,* the Blessed Virgin gave Maria Cruz a practical lesson on how to recite the Creed, the Hail Holy Queen and the Sign of the Cross on August 8,

[1] See paragraphs 12 and 13, and see also *The Constitution on the Church,* paragraph 67.

1961. The lesson came at the conclusion of a memorable event. The four girls had gone in an ecstatic march from the church to the pines and there had been joined in their vision of Our Lady by the Jesuit, Father Luis Maria Andreu. Not only was Father Luis the only person to have ever seen Our Lady at Garabandal besides the four girls, but, on this same occasion when he participated with them in the vision at the pines, he was also granted a privilege that they never had, namely, a preview of the great miracle that is yet to come. From the pines, the four girls went in ecstasy to the church. There the vision ceased for all of them, except Maria Cruz, who, still in ecstasy, entered the church where she received her instruction in private prayer. Conchita describes the lesson as follows:

When she [Maria Cruz] arrived at the altar of Our Lady of the Rosary and of the archangel Saint Michael, she started to say the Creed *very slowly* with the Blessed Virgin. Maria Cruz said that the Blessed Virgin took the lead and recited the prayer first, in order to teach her to pray *slowly.* After the Creed, she said the Hail Holy Queen and then she made the Sign of the Cross *very slowly* and *very properly— muy despacio, muy bien* (Emphasis added).

In the same *Diary,* Conchita tells us that ten days later, on August 18, Our Lady gave the same kind of practical lesson in prayer to the four girls together. This time the rosary was the object of her simple motherly instruction.

. . . The Blessed Virgin appeared to us again. The first thing she told us was to say the rosary. As, naturally, we never took the lead in reciting it, she said to us: "I am going to pray first and you will follow me." And she recited the prayers *very slowly—muy lento*. She said "Holy Mary" and we repeated "Holy Mary." We prayed in that manner. When it was our turn to say: "Hail Mary" and the other parts of the rosary prayers, we said them very slowly. When we came to the Hail Holy Queen, she told us to sing it and we did. At the end of the rosary, she gave us a kiss and departed . . . (Emphasis added).

In April of 1969, Conchita was sent a series of questions, several of which dealt with the rosary. One of them was the following: "Did Our Lady continue to say the rosary with the girls in ecstasy, even after they had learned to say it the way she wanted?" Conchita's reply: "After the first day, she no longer recited it. But when the time came for the Gloria, she indicated it to us by bowing her head." At Lourdes, the Blessed Virgin never recited the Hail Mary with Bernadette as the child said the rosary, but it has been stated that she did say the Gloria with her.

Through another one of these questions it was learned that after the girls had been taught to say the rosary by the Blessed Virgin they continued to say it that way, "but when they did not see her they did not recite it so slowly."

Our Lady Commands Recitation of Rosary

Still other questions brought out the additional information that at each apparition Our Lady "commanded" the girls to recite the rosary, a thing they "always" did.

It was also learned through this same source that although the Blessed Virgin never preached or "talked about" the rosary to the girls, she "demanded that it be recited each day—*mando rezarle diaria-mente.*" In fact, through the *Diary* and letters written by the girls we find that Our Lady sometimes gave very precise instructions regarding when and where the rosary was to be recited. Describing an apparition that occurred in the early days of November, 1961, Conchita writes in her *Diary:*

> The Blessed Virgin ordered—*mando*—the four of us, Loli, Jacinta, Maria Cruz and myself, to recite the rosary at the *cuadro* (a protective wooden enclosure in the *calleja* or sunken lane at the exact spot where all of the early apparitions took place). On certain days we went at six o'clock and on others at a later hour. Jacinta and Maria Cruz went at six o'clock in the morning and at seven. Loli did not go at any fixed time. Later, Maria Cruz was not able to get up so early and she went at eight o'clock, while Jacinta went at six with her mother. People from the village went with us. During Holy Week, the Blessed Virgin ordered us to go at five in the morning, which I did because the Blessed Virgin always wanted us to do penance.

That Conchita remembers and notes all these details concerning the various hours at which the girls recited the rosary at the *cuadro* indicates how important she considered Our Lady's command to be.

Conchita in her *Diary* does not explicitly state that Our Lady herself ordered these early hours, except for Holy Week. But it is implied and indeed this is clearly stated in a letter which Maria Cruz wrote to Father José Ramon Garcia de la Riva on January 11, 1962: "Yes, I go to say the rosary every day at six in the morning. The Blessed Virgin commanded me—*me le mando la Virgen*—to recite

it at that hour every day until I start seeing her
again." (Our Lady had told Maria Cruz in November of 1961 that she would not see her again until
January 16, 1962.).

Penitential Recitation

The thought behind the early hour and the open
air recitation of the rosary is quite evidently to make
the children and those who accompanied them practice penance. In fact, Conchita mentions this when
speaking of the five o'clock recitation requested by
Our Lady for Holy Week. She states that she herself
complied with that "order." Jacinta also seems to
have been very generous in this regard, as evidenced
by the following statement she made to the same Don
José Ramon in a letter which she wrote on October
19, 1962, almost a year after Our Lady's original
request: "I had an apparition of the Blessed Virgin
at eight [in the evening] after the rosary and then I
had another at four [in the morning], and I am writing to you now because I am waiting for six o'clock
to go and say the rosary at the *cuadro*."

From all these various remarks it is easy to understand how Conchita could say in reply to another question asked in April, 1969: "Yes, the rosary
is a very important part of the Blessed Virgin's message."

Other Private Prayers Recommended

In speaking of the private prayer message of
Garabandal, it should also be mentioned that Our
Lady recommended visits to the Blessed Sacrament.
This, like the general recommendation "to be good"
and the need to pray for priests, is something that
she came back on very often in her visits with the

girls. She also requested that we "think of the passion," which is quite interesting for we border here on a higher form of prayer than simple vocal prayer, namely, meditation. It is significant that Our Lady used the word "think" and not meditate. She evidently wanted to reach as many souls as possible and did not want to frighten any one with the word "meditate" which, for most people, has mysterious and sophisticated connotations. She was inviting us to reflect on or to think about the passion, something that everyone can do.

Analysis of Vocal Prayer Recommendations

It is important to return now to Our Lady's specific recommendations regarding the manner of saying vocal prayers. There is much more to these recommendations than appears on the surface. The Blessed Virgin was really trying to tell us some very important things in her simple instructions to the girls.

Tape Recordings Are Most Informative

Not only do we know the precise pedagogical procedure used by Our Lady in teaching the children how to say the rosary and other vocal prayers—leading them herself, pronouncing a few words at a time, then having the children repeat these after her—but we know the end product. Tape recordings were made of these prayers at Garabandal during the apparitions. There is one recording of Jacinta reciting the rosary and the act of contrition in ecstasy and of Conchita saying the rosary in ecstasy. These are samples of the finished product, so to speak, of Our Lady's instructions to the children regarding the recitation of vocal prayers.

It is very apparent from this tape that the Blessed

Virgin taught the girls two things: pronounce each word of the vocal prayers very slowly and distinctly, and make a distinct and perceptible pause after each meaningful group of two or more words.

Here is a detailed description of the first part of the Hail Mary as recited by Jacinta and Conchita in ecstasy according to the tape mentioned above. The second part of the prayer is answered by the spectators present at the apparition. It takes the girls from 20 to 24 seconds to say from the first words "Hail Mary" to the last ones "womb, Jesus," and there are six clearly marked pauses between various short groupings of words. Translated into English, the Spanish tape comes through approximately as follows: "H-a-i-l M-a-r-y . . . f-u-l-l o-f g-r-a-c-e . . . t-h-e L-o-r-d i-s w-i-t-h t-h-e-e . . . b-l-e-s-s-e-d a-r-t t-h-o-u . . . a-m-o-n-g w-o-m-e-n . . . a-n-d b-l-e-s-s-e-d i-s t-h-e f-r-u-i-t . . . o-f- t-h-y w-o-m-b J-e-s-u-s.

Deliberate Recitation

The purpose of this detailed description of the tape recording is not to give an example for slavish imitation. Our Lady is not concerned with any definite amount of time, any counting of seconds. The description was given to illustrate the basic principle of deliberateness, which is what the Blessed Virgin was trying to teach us.

Our Lady was certainly not trying to set down an absolute and unchangeable time pattern that everyone should necessarily follow. She was simply trying to tell us that we have to slow down the recitation of our vocal prayers, slow it down enough so that we can make it really meaningful. That is the whole reason behind the deliberateness.

Three Elements in Prayer—Role of the Will

For practical purposes we can distinguish three things in prayer; the will to pray, the use of our mind, and of our heart. The will to pray is the most important element. If it is there, our prayer will always have some value, no matter how far our mind may stray or how dry our heart may be. Willful, deliberately entertained distractions, are, of course, another thing. They do, in varying degrees, weaken or nullify our will to pray. But, if we want to pray, and actually try to pray, no matter how far our mind and heart may seem to be from God, no matter how poorly we may seem to succeed, we are truly praying and our prayer is acceptable to God. In a real sense, it is our desire and effort to pray that counts with God. It is not the fancy words that we use, or the glow and good feeling that may occasionally accompany our efforts that impress and please God. These impress and please us, not him.

But if prayer is to have real meaning for us and be fully pleasing to God, it must include more than the will to pray. The mind and the heart must also have their part in it. And this is where the deliberateness taught by Our Lady at Garabandal comes in. We cannot think and elicit love in our prayer if we race through it. We have to slow it down, and most of us have to slow it down considerably. It is as simple as that. That is what the Blessed Virgin was trying to say to us through the four little Spanish girls.

Thinking—Role of the Mind

Our vocal prayers should involve some thinking. The thinking can be about God, Jesus, Mary, or the words of the prayers we are saying, or the mysteries of the rosary, if we are reciting that prayer. But there must be some thinking, some working of our mind as we pray, not just an empty motion of our lips. This is not to say that we must meditate as we pray. Thinking can and frequently will lead to meditation, but it is not quite the same thing. We can all think, but many of us experience difficulty in meditating in the full sense of that word. Meditation implies a certain development of a thought, a pursuing of a thought. Many people find it hard to stay with a thought for any length of time, long enough to really meditate, and yet they can put thought into their prayer. They can use their minds in a simple and spontaneous way. But not if they are pouring out words at a rapid pace. There is a considerable degree of slowness required in the saying of the words if the mind is to have time to function, even in a simple way.

Thinking about What We Are Saying

To get us to put our minds to work or to "think" as we recite the rosary was definitely one of Our Lady's concerns at Garabandal. This is clearly stated by Conchita in answers she gave during October, 1969, to additional questions sent to her concerning the rosary. The first question was: "Did The Blessed Virgin speak of the meditation of the mysteries of the rosary? Her answer throws considerable light on this whole question of the slow recitation of the prayers of the rosary: "The Blessed Virgin spoke of meditating on the rosary, that is, of thinking about what we were saying—*pensar en lo que rezabamos.* However, she did not say anything in particular about the mysteries." The other follow-up question was:

"What did she say of the mysteries of the rosary?" Her answer: "Nothing."

What Our Lady sought specifically then was that we think about the prayers we are reciting, that we reflect upon the words we are pronouncing. This is an informal sort of meditation. It is not what is usually referred to as meditation on the mysteries. Conchita is quite clear on that point. The Blessed Virgin just did not bring up the matter of meditation on the mysteries. This, of course, does not mean that she does not favor it. Meditation on the mysteries is, indeed, a part of the Fatima First Saturday Devotions. It is simply that she was attempting to reach the broadest possible number of souls and therefore did not want to propose a form of prayer that would definitely be beyond the reach of some and that could easily discourage many others. She chose a middle course, knowing that what is ideal theoretically is not necessarily attainable or suitable for everyone.

We have here the striking example of the visionary of Lourdes, Bernadette. The trouble she had learning the simple answers of her catechism as a child was undoubtedly something the Lord had planned for our instruction. So, too, was the difficulty she later experienced in her prayer life even after she had entered the convent. She was never able to become proficient in meditating. The prayer by which she sanctified herself as a nun was the simple rosary recited with recollection and love.

Acts of Love—Role of the Heart

What is said of the use of the mind applies to the heart. Our hearts, sentiments of love, must enter into our prayers. These normally flow in a natural way from our thoughts. Thinking about God, Jesus, or Mary will automatically provoke sentiments of love for them. But the love will not come into speedily recited prayers, prayers that are only a rapid-fire rattling off of words.

Loving God is more important than thinking about God. So, too, in prayer, the part of the heart and of love is more important than that of the mind and of thinking. This is consoling and encouraging. There are many times, days of great fatigue, of illness, of emotional stress of all kinds, when it is impossible to think or even to keep one's mind for any time on a given topic. On these occasions, the heart can take over and fill the gap created by the practical temporary incapability or sluggishness of the mind. It will suffice to vaguely unite one's heart, to simply direct one's affections to Jesus or Mary. Here again, the slow, deliberate recitation of the vocal prayers will soothe the soul and dispose it to this fruitful and satisfying prayer of affective union with Christ and his Blessed Mother.

Our frustrations in prayer, which lead to its partial or total abandonment, come in great part from the fact that we do not put our mind and heart in it. Prayer in which the mind and heart do not participate is a dehumanized prayer which cannot possibly satisfy us. Because of the struggle between the spirit and the flesh, the carnal and the spiritual man, prayer will never be very easy. But it should be a meaningful and rewarding experience. And it will be if we put our mind and our heart in it.

Practical Pointers

Let us take a closer look at the precise form of deliberate prayer that is revealed in the tapes mentioned above. Two things were noted: a very slow pronunciation of the words and a considerable pause between groups of words. Both factors are important and contribute together toward a total tempo of prayer that is conducive to thinking and to loving God.

Vital Importance of the Pause

The substantial pause, the complete stop between the various short groups of words, is a key factor. It sets the rhythm and helps to maintain a steady slow pace. It works as a check or brake on the natural tendency that we have to speed up prayers that are repeated continually, day after day, even when they are properly pronounced.

It is especially the pause that fosters thinking and acts of love. It can be lengthened at will, as the Holy Spirit illumines our minds and invites us to dwell lovingly on certain words or thoughts. Following the impulse of his grace in our purely private recitation of the rosary is important. In group prayer, of course, a steady pace must be maintained and this cannot be too slow. But when we are alone, we shall never pray too slowly. It is much better to say one decade in a truly leisurely way, with our mind and heart really in it, than to say the full five decades at a rate of speed that allows no time for their participation.

The importance of a distinct pause or clear break in the recitation of vocal prayers cannot be stressed too much. The real success of Our Lady's formula for private prayer and the rosary depends upon it. A deliberate pronunciation of each word does not suffice, nor does a simple slowing down between groups of words. There must be a noticeable break after every few words, the exact grouping of these words not mattering that much and depending on personal preference. A few attempts at this slow, pause-interrupted prayer will reveal what Our Lady meant and was trying to tell us.

Thanks to the Holy Spirit, a continual newness and freshness will be discovered in the rosary's rich, meaningful words which tired us so when we ran through them in the past. Thanks also to the promptings of the same Spirit, sentiments of love will well up in our hearts. Holy resolves will follow. At this point, the rosary has become a true prayer.

Prophetic Message

It is interesting to note that the recent changes in the Mass and breviary have incorporated the principle of deliberateness. At Mass now, the scripture readings and the prayers recited by the priest are considerably slower and there are pauses for "thinking." The common or public recitation of the new breviary includes these same features.

And so we find that the message of Garabandal is prophetic in still another way. Our Lady took the lead in teaching us how to renew our prayer. She did so in an area she knew was vital and would be overlooked, namely, that of private prayer.

7

Practical Applications

Need of a New Attitude—Seeking Contact with God

It would seem that we need to reform our basic attitude on vocal prayer. This prayer should not be thought of in terms of acquitting an obligation, of saying a prescribed number of formulas. What we should have in mind when we engage in it is that we are attempting to enter into dialogue with God, to establish a truly personal relationship with him, to get through to him. Praying and saying prayers are not necessarily the same thing. We can say prayers without really praying. As we start our prayer, our attitude should not be: "I am going to recite so many prayers, so many Hail Marys and Our Fathers, and when I have said the number I set for myself, I shall have prayed." Rather, it should be: "I want to enter into contact with the most wonderful being that exists. I want to talk to him (or to Jesus or Mary), person to person. To help me, I shall use certain rich, meaningful prayers that will serve as a starting point, a launching pad for getting to them. My purpose is not to do a thing, but to reach God, to establish a living contact with him."

Quality rather than Quantity

In this regard it might be helpful to build our prayer life around the concept of time rather than of

quantity. Determine how much time we want to give
to prayer each day—for there should be some prayer
each day, though not necessarily in the morning or
in the evening—and forget the matter of how many
prayers we shall say. Put the accent on quality rather
than quantity by leaving the number of prayers completely open, a thing that will vary each day according to the inspiration of the Spirit.

Most of us are driven principally by considerations
of quantity. We feel that we should say certain
prayers, a definite number of prayers, the entire
rosary, for example. And we feel that if we have recited the prescribed quantity which we have deter-
mined for ourselves, all is well. We are so convinced
of the prime importance of quantity, that we rush
through these prayers with little concern for their
quality. The thing that counts is to get them said.
How we do this—in practice, if not in theory—is
not that important.

It would be so much better to say that we shall
pray for so many minutes each day and not worry
about the number of prayers we fit into that period.
So, too, for the rosary. It would be preferable to allot
an amount of time for it and to say as many decades
as a deliberate, thoughtful and loving recitation will
allow. If we prayed this way, with real meaning, we
would probably find ourselves assigning more and
more time to prayer.

The Rosary Comes to Life

All of us can benefit from a hard look at this principle of deliberateness. Those who have already
given up on the rosary or who are tempted to do so
because of the "deadly" monotony of the endless
Hail Marys, will find that a truly deliberate recita-

tion dispels monotony and infuses life-giving meaning. Those who are still reciting the rosary daily or frequently, will discover that this deliberateness invigorates their prayer and transforms it into something they never imagined was possible. All will soon come to realize that they had never really prayed before.

There is a grave danger that menaces those who say the rosary frequently. They come easily to a point where they rush through it because they have unconsciously developed a "getting it in" attitude that is strongly tinged with formalism and legalism. Most of those who say the rosary regularly do so because at some moment in their life they became convinced of its importance and took the resolution to recite it each day. They say it each day, but as time goes on they seem to become more concerned with the resolution than with the prayer, with keeping their word than with communicating with God. Too soon, the primary concern becomes "getting it in." They race through the prayer and almost sigh with relief when it is over. Hardly a real prayer!

Saint Theresa Used This Method

The saints have always sensed the need for deliberate, meaningful and loving prayer. Saint Theresa of Lisieux, the Little Flower, has a most interesting section in her autobiography, *The Story of a Soul,* that illustrates the principle that Our Lady was attempting to teach us at Garabandal. The passage in question is also quite consoling for it reveals that even at the end of her life, when her union with God had reached its peak, Saint Theresa was still human and beset with the same difficulties regarding prayer that plague us all.

I find the recitation of the rosary harder than putting on a hair shirt. I feel that I say it so badly! Try as I will to meditate on the mysteries of the rosary, I just can't keep my mind on them. . . . Sometimes, when I am in such a state of spiritual dryness that I can't draw a thought from my mind which will unite me with God, I recite an Our Father and a Hail Mary *very slowly*. Then these prayers enchant me and nourish my soul much more than if I had recited them hurriedly a hundred times. (The emphasis is Saint Theresa's.)

We, too, would do better to say one or two decades of the rosary very slowly, "à la Garabandal," rather than race through the whole rosary!

Flexibility Desirable

Saint Theresa's remarks raise the question of some possible flexibility in the recitation of the rosary. A large measure of flexibility and adaptability is both necessary and fully in keeping with what Our Lady was trying to tell us at Garabandal about avoiding excessive formalism in prayer. Each person should attempt to find the precise formula of private prayer that best suits him, that is, the one best tailored to his particular needs, which is not the same, of course, as his whims and fancy. For example, a person who is very nervous, or sick or weak, or who for any reason finds it difficult to pray for a sustained period of time, will undoubtedly pray the rosary more fruitfully by dividing it up and reciting it a decade or two at a time, and he should not hesitate to do this.

Choosing a Time to Pray

Also, whether you say the five decades of the rosary without interruption or only one or two at a time, it is very important to determine and set aside the moments of the day or the evening that experience has shown to be most appealing to you and most conducive to devout prayer. Private prayer is so vital that we must take every human means to assure its fervent recitation and our fidelity to it.

We must recognize the fact that there are moments in the day when we are so preoccupied or tired that we don't feel like praying and simply cannot pray well. For most of us, if we wait until the very end of the day, we find ourselves so tired and eager to get into bed that we are just not in a suitable frame of mind to pray, let alone pray slowly and deliberately. Lack of discernment and proper planning is one of the major reasons why so many people pray poorly, fail to devote sufficient time to private prayer, and eventually come to abandon it almost completely.

If we are to persevere in private prayer and devote to it the time we should, it is supremely important that we do everything we can to make it as humanly appealing as possible. For grace builds on nature. And prayer will always be difficult enough without making it more difficult than necessary by the poor time we choose for it.

With good will and a little experimentation we shall come to discover a definite period of time each day when we find it relatively easy to pray and to pray well. This we should reserve for God and defend jealously. This is the precious pearl in comparison to which nothing else has value and for which we should be willing to sell all else. This is the leaven that will raise and transform our lives, giving them direction and meaning and bringing us peace and joy.

Broader Prayer Lessons of Garabandal

In addition to the various specific things that have been said about the rosary message of Garabandal, there are still some other broad and important lessons to be drawn, not from Garabandal alone but from Lourdes and Fatima as well.

The Need of Private Prayer in Our Daily Lives

First, as the rosary is a form of private prayer and was recommended at all three places, it would seem legitimate to conclude that Our Lady was trying to tell us through the striking medium of heavenly visions that we should put private, personal prayer into our daily lives.

Somehow we continually need to be reminded—and occasionally in a dramatic way through apparitions—that we must "pray always." For our truest posture in the face of God our Father, is that of children with outstretched hands.

The girls recited the rosary as they walked in ecstasy to the pines, to the cemetery, around the church, through the village streets, and when visiting the sick in their homes. This can be seen as an invitation to us to say the rosary as we walk about, wait for a bus, drive our car, etc. As so often happened at Garabandal, Our Lady taught us through the actions of the girls in ecstasy as much as through her verbal recommendations.

When we do not have time to say the rosary, or even a decade, we can still discover many moments each day when it is easy to recite one or more deliberate Our Fathers or Hail Marys, for example, while shaving or putting on makeup, while walking from one room or office to another, while doing any number of simple actions that do not absorb our mind and leave it free to "think about what we are saying." By spacing prayer in this way throughout our day, we will create a mentality or habit of prayer and recollection that will be most helpful and rewarding.

Private prayer and frequent private prayer, were certainly things the Blessed Virgin was trying to teach us at Garabandal. But most of all, she wanted to impress upon us the need for praying well and not simply going through the motions, whether it be the rosary or some other form of private prayer. As seen above, she taught Maria Cruz to say the Creed and the Hail Holy Queen "very slowly", and to make the Sign of the Cross "very slowly and very properly." A delightful childish incident related to the ecstasies will bear out how concerned Our Lady was with this. The ecstasies generally ended in this manner: the girls kissed Our Lady on each cheek, made the Sign of the Cross, lowered their heads and then simply returned to their normal condition. Conchita, to delay Our Lady's departure, would at times deliberately make an imperfect Sign of the Cross and repeat it several times. It was only when she had finally made it properly, that Our Lady would depart.

The Power of the Rosary—Good Pope John

Also, since the private prayer most strongly recommended at Lourdes, Fatima and Garabandal was the rosary, it is quite evident that the Blessed Virgin was reminding us of her unique power of intercession among the saints. She was attempting to tell us that we need the help that this power can provide and she was graciously inviting us to have recourse to it.

Good Pope John, who called Vatican II, was a

man who believed with his whole heart in the power of the rosary and who through that prayer was drawn to Jesus in the Blessed Sacrament. He would have been dismayed had he lived to witness the decrease of devotion to Our Lady, the rejection of the rosary and the decline of faith in the Divine Presence that followed in the Council's wake. There is hardly a page in his spiritual diary, *Journal of a Soul,* that does not speak of Mary. The two great devotions of his life that stand out in this document are the rosary and the Eucharist, and the Eucharist in its full dimension of Mass or sacrificial banquet and Divine Presence in the tabernacle. He states explicitly in the *Journal* that one of the great consolations of his life is the fact that he has always been faithful to the daily rosary. As Bishop and later as Pope, he recited the rosary each evening with his entire household staff of laity, priests, and nuns. When he was named Cardinal Patriarch of Venice with pastoral responsibilities for souls he felt the need for more prayer and resolved "to recite all fifteen decades of the rosary every day, if possible in the chapel before the Blessed Sacrament" (p. 23).

Smile and Kiss of Approval

Bernadette has left us a moving description of the first apparition at Lourdes. Here are the most significant parts of that description: "I saw a Lady in white . . . I was afraid . . . I put my hand in my pocket. I took out the rosary which I always carry with me . . . I recited the rosary . . . When I finished my rosary, she greeted me with a smile."

Our Lady's smile at Lourdes, her kiss at Garabandal, these were the symbols of her approval of the rosary, the prayer that led Bernadette to sanctity, that left such a deep spiritual imprint on the lives of the children of Fatima and that is recited so faithfully each day by the girls of Garabandal. Her smile, her kiss, her help await all those who recite the rosary properly, with meaning and love.

"The rosary is a very important part of Our Lady's [Garabandal] message," Conchita has said. It is important because of the treasures of grace that it will unlock for us. It is important also as a means of keeping our devotion to Mary alive and effective. Without it, or some other adequate substitute which is still to be found, she will soon fade from our minds and from our hearts. Devotion to her cannot survive in a vacuum. It must be sustained and nurtured by prayer. That, too, is one of the things Mary was trying to tell us at Garabandal when she told the girls to say the rosary every day.

There was great insistence at Garabandal on the Eucharist and particular stress was placed on visiting Our Lord in the Blessed Sacrament. It is in the village church that the people of Garabandal gather each day to say the rosary. Isn't Our Lord also trying to tell us something through this fact? Aren't our churches the place where we should attempt to say the rosary as often as we can?

8

The Scapular and Kissed Objects

Scapular and Rosary Go Together

For centuries the wearing of the scapular has been closely associated with the recitation of the rosary. These have long been considered as sister practices that go together. Children were enrolled in the scapular and given a rosary on the day of their first solemn Communion. It is not surprising then to find them both mentioned in each of the three great Marian apparitions of modern times.

At Lourdes, Our Lady appeared eighteen times to little Bernadette in 1858. Her first apparition was on February 11 and the last one was on July 16, the feast of Our Lady of Mount Carmel. That Our Lady chose to end her visits at Lourdes on that day is not without significance. It was a silent but obvious preaching of the scapular, just as her preaching of the rosary had been silent but eloquent. Our Lady did not say a word to Bernadette during this final appearance. But she did give a message to her and to us by choosing the feast of the scapular for her last visit. This silent message was like a last testament, something that she kept until the very end because she wanted to impress us with its importance. The scapular is the symbol of Mary's love and protection and it summarized the whole purpose of her many appearances at Lourdes. Her last visit on the feast of Mount Carmel was an invitation to wear the scapular as a symbol of our placing ourselves under her protection.

At Fatima, the scapular was kept until the end also. It was the very last thing that Our Lady recommended at the conclusion of her final apparition on October 13, 1917. As the people stared in amazement at the promised miracle, the dance of the sun, Lúcia witnessed a series of tableaux close to the base of the sun. The last of these was an apparition of Our Lady of Mount Carmel. Our Lady had twice promised the children that she would come as Our Lady of Mount Carmel.

Our Lady of Mount Carmel

At Garabandal, even greater prominence was given to the scapular. It is the very title by which Our Lady chose to identify herself. On July 1, 1961, the archangel Michael, who until then had been the only one to appear at Garabandal, said to the four girls: ". . . Tomorrow, Sunday, the Virgin Mary will appear to you as Our Lady of Mount Carmel." She did in fact appear on July 2, feast of the Visitation, "with the scapular on the right wrist." It was a brown scapular and very large. In her subsequent apparitions the Blessed Virgin usually appeared with the scapular hanging from her wrist.

Why the Feast of the Visitation?

It is legitimate to ask why Our Lady should have chosen the feast of the Visitation for her first appearance as Our Lady of Mount Carmel. The answer could be that the scapular and the feast of the Visitation both have the same general significance. The scapular is a symbol of Mary's love and protection, of her willingness to help the children confided to her by Jesus at the foot of the cross. She showed this same love and willingness to help when she visited her cousin Elizabeth who was awaiting the miraculous birth of her child, John the Baptist.

Many Graces

Although the special grace of the brown scapular of Mount Carmel is Mary's assurance to the wearer of dying in God's friendship, innumerable cures, conversions and other graces of a spiritual nature have been obtained through this sacramental. The nineteenth century French Jesuit, Blessed Claude de la Colombière, has well summarized the long history of this particularly efficacious sacramental when he said: "No devotion has been confirmed with miracles more numerous and more authentic."

Invitation to Wear the Scapular

In assuming the title of Our Lady of Mount Carmel at Garabandal, and by holding out the scapular to us, as it were, by carrying it frequently at her wrist, the Blessed Virgin was telling us that it still pleases her that we wear her mantle and that she will continue to bless and protect in a special way those who do this with faith and confidence. Our Lady even seemed to be telling us something by the very size of the scapular she carried. It was unusually large, similar in size to the maniple that the priest formerly wore at Mass over his left arm. It was as though the Blessed Virgin wanted to be sure that we would not fail to notice the scapular, as though she was trying to impress us in this concrete way with the importance she attaches to it.

Objects Kissed by Our Lady

The love that Mary manifests to those who live under the mantle of her scapular, she also shows to her children through the medium of the "kissed objects" so particular to Garabandal. The kissed objects of Garabandal and their distribution to their rightful owners is one of the more intriguing aspects of these contemporary Spanish apparitions.

The kissing of objects started early in the apparitions but was considered so vital by the Blessed Virgin that she made it the principal object of her very last visit at Garabandal on November 13, 1965, and she told Conchita in advance that she would come for that purpose. "It was to be a special apparition," Conchita writes, "to kiss religious objects that would be distributed afterwards, for they have great importance." Conchita has written a report of this apparition.

The following are the significant parts of the report:

> She said to me: "You will recall what I told you on your patronal feast [the Immaculate Conception, December 8], that you would suffer much on earth. Well, have confidence in us and offer your suffering generously to our Hearts for the welfare of your brethren. In this way, you will feel how close we are to you."
>
> And I said to her: "How unworthy I am, dear Mother, of the numerous graces I have received through you. And yet, you come to me today to lighten the little cross that I now carry."
>
> She replied: "Conchita, I have not come for your

sake alone. I have come for all my children, so that I may draw them closer to our Hearts."

Then she said: "Give me everything you have brought so that I may kiss it."

I gave her everything. I had a crucifix with me. She kissed that also and said: "Place it in the hands of the Child Jesus." This I did. The Child did not say anything to me.

After having kissed everything, she said to me: "Through the kiss I have bestowed on these objects, my Son will perform prodigies. Distribute them to others."

"I will be glad to do this," I replied.

She asked me to tell her about the petitions that people had requested I transmit to her.

And I told her about them.

Then she said: "Talk to me, Conchita, talk to me about my children. I hold them all beneath my mantle."

"It is very small, we can't all get under it," I replied.

She smiled: "Do you know, Conchita, why I did not come myself on June 18, to deliver the message for the world? Because it hurt me to give it to you myself. But I must give it to you for your own good, and if you heed it, for the glory of God. I love you very much and I desire your salvation and your reunion here in heaven with the Father, the Son and the Holy Spirit. We can count on you, Conchita, can we not?"

"If I were to see you continually, I would say, yes. But, if not, I don't know, because I am so bad," I answered.

"You do everything that you can, and we will help you."

She stayed only a very short while.

"This will be the last time you see me here—*Sera*

la ultima vez que me vea aqui. But I shall always be with you and with all my children," she said.

She also said to me: "Conchita, why do you not go more often to visit my Son in the tabernacle? He waits for you there day and night."

I told the Blessed Virgin: "I am happy when I see both of you. Why don't you take me now to heaven with you?"

"Remember what I told you on your patronal feast day," she replied. "When you present yourself before God, your hands must be filled with good works done for your brothers and for His glory. But at the present time, your hands are empty."

It is all over now. The happy moments when I was with my heavenly mamma and my best friend [an expression frequently used by Conchita] and the Child Jesus, have passed. I have ceased seeing them, but I have not stopped feeling their presence.

Once again, they have left my soul filled with peace and joy and a great desire to overcome my faults and to love with all my strength the Hearts of Jesus and Mary that love us so much. . . .

P.S. (This is something that I am affirming on my own—*Esto lo digo yo.*) There is no use believing in the apparitions, if we do not comply with the message, or rather, if we do not comply with what Holy Mother Church asks of us.

The miracle is going to take place so that we will fulfill the message and also to confirm these apparitions. However, if we fulfill the message, it doesn't matter if we don't believe in the apparitions.

Unusual Phenomenon

At first, the thought of the Blessed Virgin kissing objects seems strange, and is almost upsetting. It is the first time in the annals of Marian apparitions that a thing of this kind has happened, and the new always seems strange, especially in matters such as these. However, a little historical investigation into this unusual phenomenon brings to light a number of revealing facts.

Many Marian apparitions involve sacramentals of one kind or another. The rue du Bac gave us the Miraculous Medal with its promise of "great and abundant graces for those who wear it with faith." A number of other apparitions have centered around a scapular, starting with the brown scapular given to Saint Simon Stock in 1251 with its promise of a happy death to those who wear it faithfully, and passing through the nineteenth century green scapular of the Immaculate Heart with its assurance of special graces for the conversion of sinners.

Lourdes and Fatima both have water that was discovered at the sites of the respective apparitions and which has been instrumental in bringing about cures, conversions and other spiritual favors.

Purpose of the Kissed Objects

The kissed objects of Garabandal must be viewed in this perspective. Like the scapulars and the Lourdes and Fatima water, they serve several purposes. They prove God's and Mary's love for us through the favors granted. The more exceptional favors, insofar as they apparently exceed the known forces of nature, serve both to prove the divine or supernatural origin of the apparitions and their accompanying message and to arouse and maintain interest in them. "Prodigies," whether of a physical or spiritual nature, are always the signs that authenticate supernatural events, including apparitions. Both the Old and New Testament bear abundant witness to this. In regard to Garabandal, it would appear that the kissed objects and resulting favors were meant by God to be one of the principal means for maintaining and spreading belief in the apparitions during the wait for the miracle that is yet to come.

Sacramentals

It would seem that the kissed objects of Garabandal, like the various medals and scapulars, and the Lourdes and Fatima water, are in the nature of sacramentals. They are all, at least in the broad sense of the word, "blessed" objects or material things through which it pleases God to grant favors or graces, temporal and spiritual. To be sure, God does not need these things, but he has chosen to use them. Whatever some may think of them, their acceptance by the great majority of the faithful indicates that they are admirably suited to man's psychological nature. Humility would suggest that we recognize the wisdom of the divine design and decision.

Admittedly, sacramentals at first glance seem almost childish. They also can easily lead to superstition. Yet, all this is really beside the point. The point is, does God want them, has he provided a place for them in his saving plan? "By their fruit, you shall know them," is the Christ-given test which will provide our answer. The innumerable authentic favors, great and little, that have come through the reverent and confident use of scapulars, Lourdes and Fatima water, and the kissed objects of Garabandal, give us an irrefutable affirmative reply.

Sacramentals, with their undeniable benefits, have, like so many other things, come under the fire of criticism and have tended to be discredited in our day. Through the kissed objects of Garabandal, God was telling us to maintain our faith in sacramentals and not to neglect their use. God will always distribute his grace in a way that confounds the proud in the conceit of their heart. And he will do great things for the lowly who do not question his ways.

According to *Conchita's Diary,* the kissing of objects by the Blessed Virgin (the angel never kissed them) started in the very first days of the apparitions. It continued all during the apparitions, right up to the end. It is significant that the very last of the Garabandal apparitions on November 13, 1965, was especially devoted to the kissing of objects. Our Lady had even advised Conchita in advance that this November 13, 1965, vision would "be a special apparition to kiss religious objects that I would distribute, for they have great importance."

"Prodigies"

The first "prodigies" resulting from kissed objects occurred at Garabandal while the apparitions were still going on. Many of these involved some form of clairvoyance. It was a rather frequent occurrence to have people pass objects to the children while they were in ecstasy so that they could present them to the Blessed Virgin and have them kissed by her. They took these from people in the crowd with their eyes glued on the vision and without any idea who they belonged to. They offered them to be kissed and then, with their eyes still ecstatically fixed upon Our Lady, they forced their way through several rows of spectators and returned them without fail to the proper people. Sometimes the girls returned medals on chains in this way. They opened the clasps in ecstasy, without looking at what they were doing, slipped the chains around the neck of the rightful owners and closed the clasps.

In Spain, the wedding ring is not worn on the same hand in all areas of the country. The girls would invariably go to the person in the crowd who owned the ring and slip it on the right finger of the proper hand, according to the region from which the person came. And always they would do all this with great precision, although their head and eyes were raised in ecstasy toward the vision during the entire procedure.

After the first days during which Our Lady kissed pebbles, only objects with a religious connotation were kissed by her. She kissed wedding rings because they are blessed and are associated with a sacrament, but she did not kiss ordinary rings worn simply for adornment.

One day Conchita was expecting an apparition and was waiting in the kitchen of her home for Our Lady's arrival. Other people were present and they placed various objects on the table for her to have Our Lady kiss. One of these was a fancy powder compact. There was some concern manifested by Conchita and others because of the worldly nature of the object, but the compact stayed on the table. When the apparition began, Conchita, to the spectators' amazement, went immediately and picked up the compact and presented it to Our Lady. At the conclusion of the vision, Conchita explained that the Blessed Virgin had simply said to her: "Give me that, it is my Son's." It was subsequently learned that during the Spanish Civil War the compact had been used to bring Communion secretly to prisoners of the

Reds who were destined to die. Another similar incident occurred involving an old pill box.[1]

Innumerable Graces

The list of the "prodigies," to use Our Lady's own word, that have been performed by Jesus through objects kissed by his Mother at Garabandal, is most impressive. Any attempt to evaluate their number would be pointless. It would also be impossible, for these graces, both spiritual and temporal, have been literally innumerable and their number grows each day. If just the favors received by people who have venerated the "kissed" medal presented for veneration by Joey Lomangino after his talks on the apparitions were described, it would require a book of considerable size. But there are many other persons in this country who have kissed medals and the list of "prodigies" reported by them is also very long.

Extraordinary Cure

It is beyond the scope of this book to go into any great detail concerning these reported prodigies. However, as an illustration of what is happening today, one recent case is herewith submitted. It was chosen because enough information is available to allow anyone who is so minded to check it out directly himself. The case was reported in a letter dated September 4, 1968, and sent to Father M. Laffineur,

[1] Objects kissed by Our Lady have quite frequently given off a temporary sweet scent, like that of perfume. This normally lasts a few seconds, from ten to twenty or so. It has been experienced by people singly and collectively. It was never mentioned by Our Lady to the girls, but is a well established fact. This odor of perfume or of "roses" is a rather frequent phenomenon and has been very often reported in connection with Padre Pio, the recently deceased Capuchin stigmatist.

Ncuillé, 49 Vivy, France by Professor Lucio Zumel
Menocal (Comunidades, 6,4° A, Valladolid, Spain).
Here is the letter translated by the author from Father
Laffineur's French translation of the same:

It will be a month since Dr. Cuadrado, professor
and Rector of the University of Salamanca, performed
a cancer operation on a forty-four year old lady, wife
of a doctor and daughter of a doctor.

When the operation was over, the operating surgeon
admitted to the family that he had not been able to do
anything, that the entire abdomen and all the body of
the sick lady was cancerous, that there was no possibility of any relief and that the woman would die soon
since there was no hope of a cure.

Two or three days later, the lady's family, thanks to
the Civil Governor of Salamanca and other important
personages, transferred the sick woman to Madrid and
the clinic of Social Security of Puerta de Hierro,
room 109.

This clinic deals with hopeless and extremely grave
cases. . . .

When I learned of the seriousness of the case, I
gave a nephew of the sick woman the "reliquary" [a
footnote explains that the reliquary contained a parcel
of an image or of a page of a missal belonging to Loli
and kissed by Our Lady at Loli's house] which you
sent me along with a book written by Sanchez-Ventura
and an image of Our Lady as she appeared at Garabandal. I requested that they apply the reliquary and
that everyone implore the miraculous intercession of
the Blessed Virgin.

On the important Marian feast of August 15, they
did as I had requested. As I had suggested, the father
of the young man to whom I had given the reliquary,
applied the reliquary himself to the sick woman and
told the woman and her family about Garabandal, a
name unknown to all these people.

At that time, the sick woman was not speaking, seemed to be in her death agony and the family had already begun to talk of arrangements for her burial, etc. And the man who applied the medal went to church to attend Mass. . . .

When he returned, the sick woman was talking with everyone in an almost normal way.

The next day, she got out of bed.

The day after that, she walked in the room.

The following days, she walked in the garden of the clinic.

On Sunday, she took a walk in Madrid.

The inflamation of the abdomen has disappeared, the wounds have healed and we are faced with a wonderful miracle, for without that [medal and prayers], the lady would have been buried many days ago.

The doctors are amazed.

Parting Message of Love

The deep meaning of the kissing of objects and the resulting "prodigies" is their message of love. A tender note of motherly love and concern permeated the entire final Garabandal apparition of November 13, 1965 in which Our Lady stressed these kissed objects: "Conchita, I have not come for your sake alone. I have come for all my children, so that I may draw them closer to our Hearts. . . . Talk to me about my children. . . ." The promised prodigies were meant above all to be continued proofs of Mary's love for her children at a critical time of history when it would be important for them to know that she had not forgotten them and that her power to help them was as efficacious as ever.

9

The Eucharist

Mary Leads to Jesus and the Eucharist

In reading about apparitions involving Our Lady, there is an inherent danger of focusing too much attention on Our Lady, of overstressing the Marian content of the message she brings to us from God. Since it is Our Lady who comes and speaks in God's name, it is quite understandable that we center our attention on her. But Mary's mission was and continues to be, to bring Jesus to us. It is interesting to read the story of Marian apparitions in this light. One readily discovers that Our Lady is usually trying to direct our attention not only to Jesus in a general way, but more particularly to Jesus in the Eucharist.

Eucharistic Overtones of
Miraculous Medal Apparitions

The first great Marian apparitions of the modern era occurred in Paris in 1830. They involved a simple peasant girl, Catherine Labouré, since canonized. Our Lady appeared three times to her in a convent at the "rue du Bac."

Most people identify "the rue du Bac" with the Miraculous Medal, and rightly so. The Medal did originate there. But what many do not realize is that there were very strong eucharistic overtones both to the apparitions that gave us the Medal and to the events immediately leading up to the apparitions.

Before Our Lady appeared at the rue du Bac, Catherine Labouré was favored with frequent visions of Our Lord in the Blessed Sacrament. She saw Our Lord in this way over a period of eight to nine months. This is the eucharistic backdrop for the apparitions of the Blessed Virgin, which all occurred subsequently in the rue du Bac chapel, on the steps of the main altar and before the tabernacle.

At the rue du Bac, the Blessed Virgin told Catherine "to come and kneel at the foot of the altar and to open her heart there, and that she would receive all the graces—*toutes les consolations*—she needed." She also said that ". . . at the foot of the altar, graces would be granted to all persons asking for them with confidence and fervor and that they would be showered on the great and the small alike."

Eucharist Involved at Lourdes

At Lourdes, Our Lady asked that people come in procession and that a chapel be built. Here again, the Mother of Jesus was leading her children to her Son, whose sacrifice is daily renewed on the altars of our churches and who dwells day and night in their tabernacles. The eucharistic implications of these two requests made to Bernadette have been so well understood that at Lourdes processions with the Blessed Sacrament in front of the rosary chapel have become one of the main features of the religious services daily conducted there during the pilgrimage season.

More Prominence Given to Eucharist at Fatima

At Fatima, the Eucharist was given even more prominence. An angel appeared to Lúcia, Francisco and

Jacinta three times in 1916. The last of these apparitions was almost entirely eucharistic. The angel appeared with a chalice and a Host, and he taught the children the following prayer:

> Most Holy Trinity, Father, Son, Holy Spirit, I adore you profoundly and offer you the most precious Body, Blood, Soul and Divinity of Jesus Christ, present in the tabernacles of the earth, in reparation for the outrages, sacrileges and indifference by which he himself is offended. And by the infinite merits of his most Sacred Heart and those of the Immaculate Heart of Mary, I beg of you the conversion of poor sinners.

The purpose of the angel's visit was to stress eucharistic prayer and reparation, as Our Lady herself would do later. This was emphasized as he gave Jacinta and Francisco the contents of the chalice and Lucia the Host:

> Take and drink the Body and the Blood of Jesus Christ, horribly outraged by ungrateful men. Make reparation for their sins and console your God.

Communions of reparation on the first Saturday of the month, sometimes referred to as the First Saturday Devotions, were requested by Our Lady and are another important part of the eucharistic message of Fatima.

Eucharist Key Feature of Garabandal Event

The Eucharist was mentioned in both Garabandal messages. In the 1961 message, Our Lady said: "We must visit the Blessed Sacrament frequently." In 1965, the message had far broader and graver implications: "Less and less importance is being given to the Eucharist."

The great concern expressed for the clergy in the second message also has strong eucharistic overtones. The priest's most important and specifically sacerdotal function is that of minister of the Eucharist.

The Passion and the Eucharist

The mention of the passion of Jesus in the second message also has a strong eucharistic connotation, for the Eucharist is both a sacrifice and Communion. As a sacrifice it is the unbloody renewal of the sacrifice of the cross. At Holy Mass, graces acquired by the sacrifice of Calvary are made available to us, especially to those who are actually present at Mass. Christ, the victim and high priest of Calvary, continues to offer himself to his Father for us, asking that we may share abundantly in the one sacrifice, the sacrifice of Calvary. Reflection on the passion is the best possible preparation for understanding and participating in the Eucharist-sacrifice.

Holy Communion Unites Us to Christ

The Eucharist is also Communion. It is through Holy Communion that we receive the greatest share of the graces that flow from the altar. Not only do we receive these graces in more abundance through the reception of this Sacrament, but Holy Communion is itself a distinctive grace, namely, a very special personal union with Christ. This is a point that we might easily miss. Great stress is placed on Communion as the food or strength of our soul. This is true. But it is much more than that. It is the great means for achieving a personal and intimate relationship with Christ and through him with the Father and the Holy Spirit. This personal relationship is the very heart of our Christian faith.

Role of Christ God-Made-Man

Our spiritual life will be superficial and unrewarding until we come to realize that God is a personal being, intelligent and loving, who wants us to know and love him in a personal and intimate way. But God is a spirit and difficult to visualize, seemingly an abstract and remote being that could leave us cold and indifferent. That is why God brought about the incarnation, the mystery of God-made-man, Jesus Christ. In him God became tangibly alive to us. Christ is God coming down to our level, making himself knowable. It is the role of Christ to reveal God to us as well as to atone for us.

All of Christ's actions are a revelation of God. Christ's healing of the sick, his casting out devils from the possessed, his forgiving sinners, his feeding the hungry crowds, all these actions manifested God's kindness, mercy, and concern for us. Through Christ we come to see that God is a loving personal being, with all the qualities proper to a person.

Friendship with God Ultimate Goal

The purpose of God's manifesting himself as an intelligent and loving personal being is to help us establish a personal relationship with him. Religion will always be a shallow and empty shell for us, something without substance or depth, until it leads us to a truly personal friendship with God. The Son of God became man, then, to help us understand God so that ultimately we could come to deal with him on a individual basis, speaking with him and loving him as a personal being in true friendship.

Eucharist Perpetuates Christ's Presence

In God's plan, Christ had to die and leave this earth. However, in his wisdom and power he devised a means to perpetuate the presence of the Savior on earth. In the Eucharist, Christ in his humanity would become present again on earth. To be sure, it would be his glorified humanity that would be present, but it would be his true and living humanity. We would be able to say, this is the same Christ, the meek and humble Christ, who once walked through Palestine preaching his good news, curing the sick, expelling devils and comforting the afflicted. In a sense we are even more fortunate than the Jews who lived at the time of Christ. We have him in each of our churches and religious chapels twenty-four hours of each day. He is there as man as well as God, ever waiting for us. His presence in the Eucharist, for all its mystery, speaks forcefully to our minds and our hearts. It should help us to establish a personal friendship with God and truly become his children.

Garabandal Eucharistic Message is Prophetic

It was because of all the above mentioned benefits which we derive from the Mass, Holy Communion and the abiding Divine Presence, that God through Our Lady and Saint Michael focused so much attention on the Eucharist at Garabandal. This insistence on the Eucharist was prophetic because, although the causes inimical to faith and devotion to Our Lord in this sacrament had been growing considerably before 1961, spectacular weakening of eucharistic devotion has only shown itself since that time.

Saint Michael Brings Holy Communion

Saint Michael, the archangel, often brought the girls Holy Communion at Garabandal on days when Communion was not available in the village. They always had a great desire to receive Communion. It is noteworthy that the angel prepared the children over a considerable period with "unconsecrated" hosts prior to bringing them real (but invisible) Communion, and that on the first day he brought them "consecrated" Hosts, he told them to make thanksgiving after Communion and to recite with him the "Soul of Christ."

On November 13, 1965, Our Lady reprimanded Conchita: "Conchita, why do you not go more often to visit my Son in the tabernacle? He waits for you there day and night." The fact that this remark was made at the very last apparition, is undoubtedly not without significance. It was a way of impressing Conchita with the importance of Eucharistic devotion and of making sure she would not forget it. Through letters which the girls sent to Father Jose Ramon Garcia de la Riva during the period when Our Lady was appearing, it would seem that she frequently exhorted them to visit Our Lord in the tabernacle.

Miracle of the Visible Host

One event that brings out the importance of the Eucharist in the message of Garabandal is the miracle of the visible Host. The sudden appearance of a Host on Conchita's extended tongue was God's response to the girls' insistent plea for a miracle that would prove the authenticity of the apparitions. In order that this miraculous Communion from the hands of the archangel Saint Michael could serve as a sign, the angel gave Conchita prior notice that it would occur and told her to tell the people fifteen days in advance. Thanks to this, many people witnessed the miracle and pictures of it were taken. The fact that this miracle, given as proof of the visions, involved the Eucharist, rather than something else, was not without divine purpose. It was a dramatic way chosen by God to focus attention on the Eucharist.

"Station" to the Blessed Sacrament

The messages of apparitions are conveyed by events and deeds, as well as in the words spoken by the vision. If we keep this in mind, the children's keeping of the Spanish tradition of the "station" to the Blessed Sacrament becomes very enlightening. This custom, which consists of the recitation of a few Our Fathers, Hail Marys and other prayers in honor of the Blessed Sacrament, has been faithfully maintained for years in the village of Garabandal. This was brought out vividly when the angel first appeared on June 18, 1961. When the schoolmistress, Doña Serafina Gomez, had questioned the girls about the apparition, she said to them: "Well, let us go and say a station to Jesus in the Blessed Sacrament in thanksgiving," which they did.

Conchita mentions several times in her *Diary* that the girls went to pray before the Blessed Sacrament at the conclusion of an apparition. This was their normal procedure, a thing only occasionally omitted because of the late hour or some like reason.

In Ecstasy before the Blessed Sacrament

Even more significant is the fact that, in the early days of the apparitions prior to the diocesan interdiction forbidding them to enter the church while in ecstasy, the girls went to the church during various apparitions and prayed before the Blessed Sacrament. Father Jose Ramon Garcia de la Riva, pastor of Our Lady of Sorrow, Barro de Llanes (Asturias), was a witness to this on August 22, 1961. That evening, shortly after the public recitation of the rosary in the church, the girls had an apparition of Our Lady. They were outside the church at the time. Don Jose Ramon was inside, praying before the Blessed Sacrament on the first step of the altar. Here is his description of the girls coming into the church in ecstasy and praying before the tabernacle:

> The girls entered the church several times. They came and stationed themselves next to me, on the first step of the altar. I had only to turn my head slightly to observe perfectly the unfolding of these phenomena that, at first sight, seemed mystical. The girls prayed before the Blessed Sacrament and their entire exterior bearing was a thing of remarkable beauty. They prayed in a low voice with their heads tilted slightly back. They came two by two, Conchita and Maria Cruz, and Jacinta and Loli.[1]

Even after the diocesan ban, the girls were still drawn in ecstasy to the church. They walked around the edifice saying the rosary and singing the Hail Holy Queen, or they knelt before the door.

Again Our Lady used the same procedure followed with private prayer and the rosary. To her exhortation to visit the Blessed Sacrament frequently, she added the example of the girls in ecstasy.

Saying the Rosary in Church

We must always remember that at Garabandal Our Lady was really speaking to all of us through Conchita and the other girls. She was saying to us:

[1] Don Jose Ramon has released a report of his various visits to Garabandal from 1961 to 1968. A French translation of the report has been made and will be published in France. The above quotation is from this translation which was obtained through the courtesy of Gerard Suel, Cambrai, France.

"You must visit the Blessed Sacrament frequently.
. . . Less and less importance is being given to the
Eucharist. . . . Why do you not go more often to
visit my Son in the tabernacle? He waits for you
there day and night."

An excellent way to respond to this invitation and
at the same time comply with the request for the
daily recitation of the rosary, is to imitate good Pope
John and, "when possible," say the rosary "in the
presence of the Blessed Sacrament."

Heart-to-Heart Conversation

In our visits with the Blessed Sacrament, simplicity
and spontaneity should be the rule. God does not
want sophisticated thoughts, high sounding words
or prayerbook formulas from us. He prefers to hear
us speak our own language, directly from our hearts,
without frills or fancy. Prayer is really a heart-to-
heart conversation with God, an authentic conversation, wherein we express our personal thoughts in
our own words, or even without words. Short, simple
phrases will often be the best: "My God I love you
. . . I thank you for dwelling with us in our tabernacles . . . I give you my heart. . . . Take my heart
and keep it close to yours. . . . Tell me what you want
me to do. . . . " If we talk this way, Our Eucharistic
Lord will give us the power to discern his voice as
he answers us in his own mysterious way.

Visiting the Blessed Sacrament in Spirit

Getting to church is very difficult and even impossible for many. In fact, some churches are now
locked most of the day because of the danger of
vandalism or theft. But these obstacles to visiting
the Blessed Sacrament are not insurmountable. Our

words and our love can pierce the doors of churches as well as those of tabernacles. We can visit Jesus in spirit and make real contact with him in this way from our home or from our car or from the sidewalk beside the church, and we can maintain contact with him in spirit throughout the day and evening from wherever we are. "You must visit the Blessed Sacrament frequently."

Eucharist the Central Point

At Garabandal, everything converged toward the Eucharist. The ecstatic recitation of the rosary, so important a part of the Garabandal event, frequently took the girls to the church or around the church. Some apparitions began in the church, others on the church porch. The angel brought the girls Communion often and he occasionally gave it to them on the church porch. Some of the locutions, which began about April, 1963, took place in the church. The girls usually made a "station" to the Blessed Sacrament after each apparition and they manifested the greatest respect for priests. Above all there was the miracle of the visible Host. These facts, added to the mention of the Eucharist in each of the two formal messages and to Our Lady's frequent exhortations (and reproaches) to the girls about visiting the Blessed Sacrament, give meaning to the answer Conchita gave to Mr. and Mrs. Robert Froelich of New York State in October, 1968, when they asked her about "the main emphasis as given by Our Lady at Garabandal?" She said: "Devotion to the Blessed Sacrament and prayers for priests."

10

Priests

Concern for Priests

The Eucharistic message of Garabandal finds its normal complement in the great concern for priests manifested by Our Lady at that place. Indeed, the priest's primary role is as minister of the Eucharist.

"Many cardinals, many bishops and many priests are on the road to perdition and are taking many souls with them." These words delivered in Our Lady's name on June 18, 1965 by the archangel Saint Michael form part of the second message of Garabandal. It is one of the most startling of the statements made during the entire Garabandal event.

Our Lady's concern for members of the clergy who are on the road to perdition is one of two significant new elements found only in the second message. The other is the plea for "thinking" on the passion of Jesus.

Priests Mentioned at Very Beginning

Although the priesthood was not mentioned in the first message of 1961, it was talked about by Our Lady at Garabandal long before June 18, 1965. From the first days of the apparitions in 1961, the Blessed Virgin began speaking of priests and the need to pray for them. Like other elements of the

Garabandal message, it is a thing she came back upon constantly in her frequent conversations with the girls. Her solicitude for priests and her repeated requests that we pray for them made a great impression on the youngsters. Prayers for priests became one of their preoccupations and it has remained so until this day.

Girls and Villagers Pray for Priests

On November 21, 1968, a group of people had just been talking with Loli about Our Lady's appearances to the girls. They were in her father's rustic little store and snack bar. As they were leaving, they told her that they were going to the pines and they would pray there first for her. She protested and told them to pray first for priests and then for her! A little later in that same year, in December, Conchita was operated on for appendicitis in Santander. While under anesthesia she was heard to say: "We must pray for priests . . . let us pray for priests . . . how we must pray for priests!"

Those close to the girls have acquired from them this same desire to help priests. Conchita's aunt Maximina in a letter sent to Father Garcia de la Riva on November 11, 1966, affirmed: "I don't let a single day go by without praying for all priests."

It is pertinent to recall here the reply Conchita gave the Froelichs when they asked about the main emphasis given by Our Lady at Garabandal: "Devotion to the Blessed Sacrament and prayer for priests."

Garabandal Centers Emphasize Prayer for Priests

The numerous centers that are spreading the message of Garabandal in the United States have understood this and insist greatly on these two related points.

They promote Priests' Day Observances and Priests' Night Observances. They also promote evening and all night vigils of from three to nine hours' duration and one of the principal intentions recommended at these events is the spiritual welfare of priests. Also, these vigils include Mass and exposition of the Blessed Sacrament. The passion of Jesus is not forgotten and the stations of the cross are said too.

Holy Shepherds

The concern for priests shown by Our Lady (and also by Our Lord) at Garabandal is essentially positive in character. They ask us to pray for priests so that they may be holy and may fulfill their duty of leading others to holiness. The accent is on their priestly mission of leading and sanctifying souls. The words of the second message could be misleading. "Many cardinals, bishop, priests are on the road to perdition." The accent seems to be of a negative nature, as though Our Lady's main concern were to keep priests from leaving the priesthood, getting married, etc. What she is most worried about is that sinful priests are not giving the good example that is vital in leading people to live holy lives. What she particularly deplores is the fact that a sinful shepherd—priest, bishop or cardinal—deprives his flock of the effective inspiration and leadership toward holiness that it needs and that he should be giving. Her plea for priests is a plea for holy priests who will lead their people to holiness. However, expressing this concern in a negative way as Our Lady did, is more striking and more apt to provoke a prayerful response and this is what she was seeking from us.

All this was clearly stated by Our Lord to Conchita in the locution of July 20, 1963:

Concerning priests, he told me that we should pray much for them so that they may be holy and fulfill their duty properly and make others better. "May they make me known to those who ignore me, and may they make me loved by those who know but do not love me."

The priest's role as a model of holiness is even more explicitly affirmed by Conchita in an answer to a question sent to her in the fall of 1969:

Our Lady asked us to pray for priests and consecrated souls, especially for priests because she told us that the faithful would follow their example.

Charter for Priests

This positive character of the Garabandal message for priests is elaborated upon in considerable detail by Conchita in a message she wrote for a French priest who visited the village at the end of July, 1967.

What the Blessed Virgin wants of the priest.

First of all, his own sanctification. He should fulfill his vows through love of God. To lead many souls to God in any other way is difficult in our day.

May he be saintly, for love of souls in Christ.

May he occasionally seclude himself in silence to listen to God who speaks to him continually.

May he think frequently about the passion of Jesus so that his life may be more united to Christ the priest. Thus he will lead souls to penance and sacrifice and will help them to better carry the cross that Jesus asks all of us to carry.

He should speak of Mary who is the one who will most surely lead us to Christ.

He should also speak to souls and make them believe that as there is a heaven, so too there is a hell.

I believe that is what heaven wants of its priests.[1]

This program for priests is not new. Seen, however, in the context of present day trends, it could be considered a warning against secularism and activism. Wasn't Our Lady telling priests that though they must show social concern, their specific business is holiness, "the things that are of God," as St. Paul puts it? That they themselves must become holy first and that their work for the poor and underprivileged will never be fully effective unless it is permeated with priestly holiness?

Identifying Priests Wearing Lay Garb

While the apparitions were taking place, the girls could always identify a priest, even in lay clothes. They also knew how many priests were in the village at a given time. Twice the author asked Conchita in July, 1968: "Is it true that when the apparitions were going on, you could detect a priest, even if he were not wearing clerical garb?" Twice she replied: "Then, yes: now, no." Twice another question was put to her: "How was it that you could detect a priest?" Both times she shrugged her shoulders and said: "I don't know."

The counterpart of the girls' mysterious recognition of something special in the priest was the deference they manifested toward them, at times in unique ways, as often happened in the presentation of kissed crucifixes. Our Lady frequently kissed crucifixes held by the girls in ecstasy and then had them present these crucifixes for kissing to certain people she indicated among the bystanders. If the ecstasies oc-

[1] From Father M. Laffineur's Canadian lecture given on December 29, 1967. The translation is the author's own.

curred in a house with priests present, Father Garcia de la Riva says that generally the girls "presented the crucifix to them for kissing on their knees."

No Natural Explanation—Doctrinal Implications

That the girls could recognize a priest in all circumstances is one of many proofs that the events at Garabandal do not have a natural explanation.

It also has doctrinal implications. It is a corroboration of the Church's traditional belief concerning the sacramental "character" of the priesthood, the indelible "mark" that the priest receives by ordination, and which identifies him and sets him off from other men. As was also the case for most of the extraordinary phenomena at Garabandal, the girls' ability to recognize priests was given more for us than for them.

Father Luis Prototype of the Holy Priest

Since the message of Garabandal was consistently imparted through people and places and happenings as well as through the words of Our Lady, we have to ask why Father Luis Andreu should have been the only person to share an ecstasy with the girls and why he should have been granted something they never enjoyed, namely, a preview of the great miracle. The answer could be, because he was a priest and a holy priest, as indeed he was reputed to be. Our Lady could have been drawing our attention to a prototype of the good shepherd who leads his flock more by his deeds than by his words. This was the kind of priest that God wants, to whom he grants special favors and insights symbolized by the sharing in the vision and the preview of the great miracle.

11

Sin, Penance and the
Passion of Jesus

Reflection on the passion of Our Lord Jesus Christ is, with devotion to Mary and the Eucharist, another of the things that stands out in the lives of saints. Holiness, to which we are all called, consists in loving Jesus Christ with our whole heart, and this is most readily achieved by thinking about his great love for us as manifested in his sufferings and his death upon the cross.

Nothing enlightens us more concerning the evil of sin than reflection on the passion of our Blessed Savior. This explains the great horror of sin which also characterized the saints. Their constant thinking about the sufferings of Christ drew them simultaneously to Christ and away from sin.

The ultimate purpose of the message of Garabandal, and indeed of the messages of Lourdes and Fatima, is to bring us "to be good." But for many of us, this means that we must begin by turning away from sin. Conversion, change of heart, turning from sin to God, this is the basic theme and the fundamental goal of all these apparitions. In a sense, all the other parts of the Garabandal message are means directed toward that end. Prayer, the rosary, the brown scapular of Mount Carmel, the Eucharist, penance and reflection on the passion of Christ will obtain for us the divine help we need to avoid sin and become good and holy people. Each of these spiritual means brings its own particular help, its own special contribution, its own grace.

Powerful Aid against Temptation and Sin.

Thinking about the sacred passion of our Redeemer possesses a special efficacy for aiding us in our constant struggle against temptation and sin. Some years ago, Pope Pius XII deplored the fact that man today has lost the very notion of sin. Undoubtedly many factors have contributed to this. One of these is modern man's unfortunate aversion to reflection on heaven, hell and the sacred passion of Christ.

Sin, penance, and sacrifice are all closely related, and they are fully understood only in the light of heaven, hell, and the sufferings of Christ. This explains why the need for reflection on heaven, hell, and the passion were stressed by Our Lady in an apparition to Conchita on January 1, 1965. Here are Our Lady's words as reported by Conchita in a letter sent to Father Alba, S.J., of Barcelona, on December 10, 1965:

> The Blessed Virgin told me on January 1, 1965, that we Catholic Christians do not think about the other world, heaven or hell. She said that we should think about them and that if we did our lives would be united with Christ. She also said that we should think and meditate more on the passion of Jesus. We should not only do this for ourselves, but we should also see to it that others do likewise. This would bring us

close to the happiness of God and we would accept our crosses with joy and for the love of God.

The final words of the "last" message of 1965 are: "Think about the passion of Jesus." The passion was the culminating point of the life of Christ, the beacon which illuminated his entire life. It is also the guiding light that must illuminate our lives. Though reflection on heaven and hell is important and necessary, nothing is so powerful and helpful as thinking on the passion and death of Jesus.

The Stations of the Cross

There is a very simple way of implementing Our Lady's request for "thinking" about the passion and that is to adopt the practice of making the stations of the cross either at church or at home. It must be noted that the indulgences attached to the way of the cross are secondary to its main purpose which is to "think" about the sufferings which Jesus endured for love of us. This thinking is what will produce in us hatred of sin and love of Christ, and this is what we should be seeking through this practice.

One has the impression that for too many people the essential feature of the way of the cross is in reality secondary, and that their main concern is with the vocal prayers and the indulgences. This possibly explains why so many have abandoned this devotional practice. It has lost its true meaning and has become for them just another form of prayer.

Basically, the way of the cross is supposed to be a form of simple mental prayer, an easy aid for reflecting on the sacred passion and death of Jesus. It is as such that it is warmly recommended here. Considered in this way as a down-to-earth and easy method for thinking about the sufferings of Christ, it can be used at home as well as in a church. Every prayer book has short meditations or simple reflections on the various stations. The images representing the various stations are found in many prayer books and pamphlets as well as on the walls of our churches. They are very expressive and sufficient by themselves to stimulate fruitful "thinking." It should be noted that Our Lady deliberately used the word "think," because this is something that we can all do and she wanted us all to reflect on the passion of Jesus.

Reading the Story of the Passion

Reading and rereading the passion of Christ as told by each of the four evangelists is also highly recommended. This might become a weekly practice for Fridays. All the standard lives of Christ have excellent sections on the passion which can be read alone or in conjunction with the gospel readings.

Thinking about the passion of Jesus cannot be too strongly encouraged. Tremendous and truly unsuspected spiritual benefits will be derived by those who have the wisdom and courage to fulfill this very important part of Our Lady's Garabandal message. The determination to avoid sin and lead "good" and holy lives, and to "perform much penance" and "make many sacrifices" will come easily to us if we "think" often about the passion of Jesus.

Daily Duty

There are many ways to implement Our Lady's request for penance and sacrifice. There are voluntary forms of penance like those usually recommended during lent, for example, giving up for a time or just occasionally passing by, a piece of candy, sugar in the coffee, butter on the bread, a drink, a movie, a television show, etc. Even prayer, such as the rosary or the stations of the cross, involves some penance, particularly if we go to church for the purpose. Praiseworthy as this voluntary type of penance may be, it should never distract us from the essential practice of penance found in the fulfillment of our daily duties. This is what Our Lady stressed at Fatima and it should never be lost sight of. As Saint Francis de Sales said so well almost four hundred years ago, the best crosses are those that the Lord sends us. They are the ones best suited to us and that involve the least danger of pride and vainglory. Literally hundreds of distasteful, disagreeable, irksome—penitential—things, inevitably confront us each day, from the alarm clock in the morning, the nick from the razor blade and the burnt toast, through the washing of dishes and diapers and the troublesome salesmen, to the brawling children and nagging wife or husband, etc. . . . Wastefully, we let these God-sent opportunities slip through our fingers. Instead of transforming them into spiritual gold through the alchemy of willing and loving acceptance, we turn them into a liability for our soul through impatience, anger and occasional revolt against God.

What a treasure we could lay up in heaven for ourselves and others, if only we were alert enough to seize these providential opportunities for the practice of penance.

12

Obedience to the Church

Conchita goes to Santander

Obedience to the Church was one of the very important demands of the Garabandal message. Like other parts of that message it was taught more effectively through the deeds of the four girls than through words. Obedience to the Church became an issue very early in the Garabandal event. It first came to the fore when Conchita was asked to go to Santander by the diocesan authorities. In her *Diary*, Conchita says that her mother told her to ask the Blessed Virgin if she wanted her to go. Our Lady was not opposed to the trip—*"ella no me lo quita"* —is the rather unusual way Conchita reports the Blessed Virgin's reply.

Conchita actually went to Santander on about July 27, 1961, and she was questioned by Father Francisco de Odriozola and doctors Piñal and Morales. These men were all members of the diocesan commission established to investigate the apparitions. They could find nothing wrong with Conchita and allowed her to return home on August 3.

The Church Doors are Closed

Three weeks later, on August 23, the day after Don Jose witnessed the girls enter the church in ecstasy and pray before the Blessed Sacrament, the diocesan authorities issued an order forbidding them to enter the church in the future while in ecstasy. Delegated by the pastor of Garabandal to replace him in the village on August 23, Don Jose Ramon found himself obliged to stop the girls that evening from entering the church during an apparition. Here is how he describes the incident and subsequent conduct of the visionaries:

> On the night of August 23, after having recited the rosary as usual, the little visionaries went into ecstasy on the porch of the church. When Loli and Jacinta came forward in ecstasy to pray inside the church, I was greatly moved at seeing them stop in front of me. We were placed in this fashion. I was standing with my back to the closed door and Loli and Jacinta were in front of me near the stone gateway that leads to the porch.
>
> It should be noted that the little girls did not know that I was going to close the door of the church on them. . . .
>
> The youngsters, then, were in front of me, standing in ecstasy. Loli inquired: "Why are they closing the church on us? We don't intend to do anything wrong. If they don't open it for us, we won't come back again." . . .
>
> . . . It is public knowledge that from that day on, the little girls never entered the church again while in ecstasy, respecting thereby the order of the apostolic administrator. Whenever they came in ecstasy to the church, they confined themselves to going around it with those who accompanied them. They recited the rosary or sang the Hail Holy Queen.
>
> Loli and Conchita received Holy Communion from the hands of the angel on the porch of the church, but never inside the church, and this, from the time of the interdiction onward.

Announcing the Message of October 18, 1961

These facts are sufficiently eloquent in themselves and require no comment. They are typical of the attitude of the girls toward church authorities during the entire Garabandal event. One other incident that occurred somewhat later will serve to further illustrate this.

Our Lady had told the girls to announce to the people on October 18, 1961, the message she had given them privately during an apparition on July 4, 1961. She gave them precise instructions concerning the time and place in which they were to make this public announcement. She told them that they themselves were to publicize the message at the door of the church and that the pastor, Don Valentin Marichalar, was to do likewise at the pines at ten-thirty at night. However, the commission objected to a public proclamation of the message at the entrance to the church. Also, because it was raining very hard that evening and the people had no protection from the storm, the commission asked that the message be delivered earlier. The girls complied fully on both counts. They and the pastor read the message at the pines and at an hour slightly in advance of that prescribed by Our Lady.

Witnesses to Obedience

The girls have had many occasions since these early days to practice obedience to the Church in circumstances where their compliance with the requests and orders of the clergy and hierarchy were painful and difficult. They are not allowed, for example, to pray the rosary with other people at the pines, a favorite peaceful place of prayer where many

apparitions occurred. Other even more odious re-
strictions have been imposed on them over the years.
And so, part of their mission is to give witness of
submission to the Church in matters where it would
be so easy to rationalize that the measures imposed
were unreasonable or excessive.

There is no need to elaborate on the appropriate-
ness in our day of this message of obedience to the
Church, except to say that it underlines the prophetic
element, as it were, of the message of Garabandal.
It is certainly food for thought in these turbulent
times and Our Lady is inviting us to "think" about it.

13

Saint Michael
The Archangel

God Speaks through His Messengers

God speaks to us through happenings like Garabandal in many ways, through places and events as
well as through verbal messages. He also speaks to
us through the persons he chooses to be his messengers. This is apparent in regard to the main messenger, Mary. It is also true, though less obvious, in
regard to his precursors or secondary messengers,
such as the Angel of Peace at Fatima and the archangel Saint Michael at Garabandal.

A New Phase in Modern Marian Apparitions

It should be noted that the association of an angel
with the Blessed Virgin in a major way, such as
happened at Fatima and Garabandal, marks a new
phase in modern Marian apparitions. It would also
seem to indicate the greater importance of these apparitions in God's plans. Angels have been used
often by God in the past to convey messages of special significance. In Old Testament times angels were
employed by Yahweh to entrust chosen individuals
with important divine missions. The angel of the
Lord appeared to Abraham by the oaks of Mamre,

to tell him that he would have a son by his childless wife Sarah (Gen 18). The angel of the Lord also appeared to Moses in the burning bush to send him on the important mission of setting Israel free (Ex 3). The same pattern continues in later times with Zachary and John the Baptist, and the Virgin Mary.

Reaffirming the Reality of the Invisible World

The angels at Fatima and at Garabandal are reminders of the existence of these spiritual creatures, over which a cloud of doubt now hangs in our day. Associating angels with the Blessed Virgin helps to create and reinforce the spiritual atmosphere of the other world. Reaffirming the reality of the invisible universe is precisely one of the vital purposes of events like Fatima and Garabandal.

The Special Meaning of Particular Angels

In addition to this, there is the special meaning attached to the particular angel involved in these happenings. At Fatima, an angel who called himself the Angel of Peace preceded Our Lady's coming by one year. He appeared three times to the little shepherds in 1916. That he called himself the Angel of Peace gives us reason to reflect when we consider that he appeared during World War I. It also corresponds to the fact that on July 13, 1917, the Blessed Virgin told Lucia, Francisco and Jacinta: ". . . Continue to say the beads every day in honor of Our Lady of the Rosary *to obtain peace* for the world and the end of the war, for she alone can help you."

Saint Michael and the Struggle with the Devil

At Garabandal, the first heavenly visitor to appear

was also an angel, the archangel Saint Michael. Like the angel of Fatima, he came before Our Lady did and his initial mission was to prepare the visionaries for her coming and also to help set the spiritual climate which constitutes such an important part of apparitions. But the fact that the angel of Garabandal was the archangel Saint Michael, had a special meaning. It indicated the basic theme of what was happening at this little mountain village. Saint Michael's very presence proclaimed the great spiritual drama that was unfolding on earth and of which Garabandal was to be one of the very important acts. It heralded a gigantic struggle in the world between the forces of good and the forces of evil, a renewal, on earth, of the supreme contest that had taken place in heaven between the faithful angels under the leadership of Saint Michael, and the rebellious spirits under the banner of Lucifer.

On January 25, 1959, a year and a half before Saint Michael's coming to Garabandal, Pope John XXIII announced his intention of convoking a Council for the updating of the Church. This was a call to arms for the forces of good, but it was also a tocsin for Satan. The devil would be well aware of the great benefits that could come to the Church from such a Council. He would have to redouble his efforts in order to counteract the Council's work.

By sending Saint Michael first, in advance of Our Lady, God was telling us that Satan was about to step up the pace of his activities in the world, unleashing his full fury against the Church. He was also advising us that he had prepared a celestial antidote to those diabolical efforts. Mighty Saint Michael, who had battled so effectively with the faithful angels in the past, would engage the devil and his horde again as the latter now began to increase his attacks against the People of God.

We may surmise that this was the deep meaning behind the sending of the archangel Michael. His coming signaled the dawn of a new epic struggle, an all out struggle with the forces of hell. The saintly Padre Pio was very conscious of the vigorous activity of the devil in the world today, and he spoke of it frequently in the years that preceded his death in 1968. He felt that it was important that people be warned. He knew only too well that "Satan's deepest wile is to make us believe that he does not exist."[1]

Saint Michael Bearer of Messages

On two successive Saturdays, June 24 and July 1, 1961, Saint Michael appeared with a sign under his feet, but the girls were not able to make out what it said. Later they learned the meaning of this sign. It contained the first message of Garabandal, a message which Our Lady herself finally gave the children on July 4, 1961, and which, at her request, they announced to the people on October 18 of that same year. It is interesting to note that Saint Michael bore or carried both messages of Garabandal, the first in the form of a sign and the second as Our Lady's messenger or spokesman on June 18, 1965.

Praying to Saint Michael

Besides announcing the great struggle in progress

[1] For those who might be inclined to think that the devil is a myth, we suggest the up-to-date and well documented *Evidence of Satan in the Modern World,* by Monsignor Leon Cristiani of the Catholic University of Lyons (The Mac-Millan Company, 1962).

with Satan, Saint Michael would be fighting on our side. The obvious implication is that we should have recourse to him in our prayers. Those who have taken to heart the Garabandal message understand this and pray frequently to him whom the Church has always invoked as a powerful ally in its struggle with the devil. When Pope Leo XIII ordered the special prayer to Saint Michael to be said after each low Mass, he did not mean to bolster the Mass, as it were, with an added prayer. But he did recognize the demonic influence at work in the world and he wanted to counteract it by an exorcism in the form of this invocation to Saint Michael. Some of those concerned with the implementation of the Garabandal message are using this invocation in their private prayers. Others invoke Saint Michael between the decades of their beads. And still others pray the chaplet of Saint Michael.

Our Lady was encouraging us to pray to Saint Michael when she told the girls at Garabandal that she wanted a chapel built in his honor near the pines. By doing this, she was also telling us what an important role God had assigned to Saint Michael in the Garabandal event which is so deeply involved in the present struggle against evil.

14

Modesty

Many things were said by Our Lady during the approximately two thousand apparitions at Garabandal. Much was ordinary conversation. But certainly there were a number of significant matters mentioned that are still unknown. There is a vast area here that needs to be explored.

One of the topics that requires elucidation is modesty. It forms a part of the Garabandal message, but is of minor importance compared, for instance, with the Eucharist, priests or the rosary. We have a parallel in the Fatima message. The Angel of Portugal did not mention modesty at all during his three 1916 appearances, nor did Our Lady during her six principal 1917 visits with the shepherd children. However, the latter mentioned it to Jacinta, in private apparitions to her, during which she declared, among other things, that certain styles would come which would offend Our Lord very much.

Our Lady Manifests Great Concern for Modesty

At Garabandal, modesty was not included in either of the two formal messages of 1961 and 1965. However, in a question sent to Conchita in the fall of 1969, enquiring if the Blessed Virgin had talked of modesty in dress, she replied: "Yes, she talked of this, and considerably. Several times she made us put down the folds of our dresses."[1] Here again, as she had done in regard to other matters, Our Lady joined to her exhortation a practical lesson in modesty.

More Subtle Teaching

The lesson of modesty was taught in other more subtle ways. Father Julio Porro Cardeñoso tells of an ecstatic fall involving Loli that he witnessed on September 8, 1961. In an ecstatic fall, the visionaries (one or several of the girls were actually involved in them), while standing or kneeling, bent slowly backward until they were fully extended on their backs, and this without hurting themselves and with their eyes always gazing upward toward the vision. Eventually, they rose by themselves to their original position. Doctor Porro observes that, given the backward tilting of her torso, Loli's dress should normally have been pulled up well above her knees. Yet he states: "Her clothes moved downward in an anti-natural movement, as though an invisible hand were assuring the girl's perfect modesty."

Father Jose Ramon Garcia de la Riva witnessed a somewhat similar happening on August 22, 1961. All four girls, while in ecstasy, fell on the floor of the village church in an unusual fall that was not the habitual ecstatic fall described above. "I noticed with astonishment," he observes in his report of the event, "that, although their fall had been precipitate, the girls' clothes remained in their normal position, covering even their knees."

Elsewhere in his report or memoirs, Don Jose Ramon says of the visionaries:

[1] *Si que hablo de esto y mucho. A nosotras nos hizo echar los dobles del vestido varias veces abajo.*

. . . I must say they were no different than the other girls of the village. They played, ran, jumped, prayed. However, in their exterior behavior they did manifest something that was not usually found in the other children, for example, in their manner of sitting down, which was always done with extreme modesty. Never at any time could they be reproached for the slightest breach of purity; their deportment in matters of purity was of the highest order. It was especially during the ecstasies that we could observe how preoccupied they were with the proper adjustment of their clothes.

While there is a practical lesson in modesty involved in these events, they have additional significance in regard to the divine origin of the apparitions. This is pointed out by Doctor Porro in this comment on the "anti-natural movement" of the girls' clothes which he witnessed: "I found this fact very significant. It was favorable evidence militating against any diabolical intervention."[1] What he is saying is that the devil is not interested in protecting or promoting virtue and would not take extraordinary measures to see that modesty is safeguarded in an event he has produced. This type of protective measure could only have God as its author and therefore points to the supernatural origin of the apparitions.

The same type of evidence against any diabolical intervention can be found in the details which Don Jose Ramon gives of the extraordinary fall of the four visionaries on the floor of the church. Loli fell first. "All the others," he affirms, "also fell on top of her, and they formed a human sculptural tableau of mar-

---

[1] *Dios en la Sombra* (Zaragoza: Editorial Circulo, 1967), pp. 88-89. The book is written under the pen name of Jose Maria de Dios.

velous beauty whose splendor and harmony I find
difficult to describe."

That a happening which normally should have
been indecorous and disorderly was just the contrary,
is an indication that the devil had nothing to do with
it. At Lourdes, after Our Lady's apparitions to Bernadette, the devil intervened a number of times and
simulated apparitions. But he always left his calling
card, and precisely in the form of grotesque and re-
volting actions on the part of the duped visionaries.[2]

[2] See Msgr Leon Cristiani's *Evidence of Satan in the
Modern World,* Chapter II, Satan at Lourdes.

15
Prophecies Already Fulfilled

Prophecies in the Strict Sense of the Word

Most of the Garabandal message was prophetic in the broad sense of the word. Doctrinal and devotional matters—the Eucharist, Mary, the rosary—which were emphasized in the apparitions would later come under attack, often very subtly, in the Church. By calling attention to these matters before they came into question, Our Lady was preparing us for the attack and in this sense the message can be defined as prophetic.

Other parts of the message are prophetic in the strict meaning of the word. Some of these specific prophecies have yet to come about while others have already been fulfilled, such as the miracle of the visible Host, mentioned above, which was announced to the people fifteen days in advance.

Prophetic Confusion among the Girls

Another important specific prophecy that has been fulfilled relates to the confusion among the four visionaries. It has to do with the doubts, denials and contradictions of the four girls concerning the apparitions. These were prophesied by Our Lady long in advance of their realization. On the same day that she predicted them, she also declared that they had

120

a symbolic meaning which was prophetic in nature. Here is how Conchita, writing in her *Diary,* toward the middle of 1963, describes Our Lady's prophecy:

> At the beginning of the apparitions, the Blessed Virgin told the four of us, Loli, Jacinta, Maria Cruz and me, that we were going to contradict each other, that our parents would not get along well with each other, and that we would come to the point where we would even deny that we had seen the Blessed Virgin and the angel. To be sure, we were greatly surprised to hear her say this to us.
>
> But in the month of January, 1963, everything that the Blessed Virgin had told us in the beginning happened. We began contradicting each other and we went as far as to deny that we had seen the Blessed Virgin. We even went to confess it one day.
>
> However, interiorly—*en nuestro interior*—we knew that the angel and the Blessed Virgin had appeared to us, because they had brought to our souls a peace, a deep joy and a great desire to love them more than ever with all our heart. . . .

It was in 1961, "at the beginning," that Our Lady made this astonishing prophecy. The girls themselves were completely bewildered, "greatly surprised," when they heard it. When, as was the custom, they were questioned at the end of the apparition and asked what Our Lady had said, they did not know what to reply. They looked at each other in a questioning manner. When urged to answer, they said that they did not understand what the vision had said. Finally they repeated the prophetic words reported above. Then they were asked if that was all that Our Lady had said. "No," they replied. "She also said: 'In this way you will establish among yourselves the same confusion that now exists in the church.' "

A priest was present at this questioning. He protested strongly: "This cannot be the Blessed Virgin appearing. It is the devil who is saying these things. There is no confusion in the Church." This protest was an indication that the full prophetic import of Our Lady's words would become apparent only later.

Contradictions and Denials

As Conchita indicated in her *Diary,* the girls did indeed come to contradict each other and deny that they had seen the Blessed Virgin. It is beyond the purpose of this book to enter into this involved matter. It will be treated in the author's forthcoming book *Our Lady Comes to Garabandal.* Let it simply be stated here that Lucia of Fatima underwent a period of doubt that lasted almost an entire month, in 1917, while the apparitions were still taking place. Then, later, at two other moments in her life, she was again assailed with doubts concerning the apparitions. Bernadette also experienced doubts concerning her visions.

Who would have dreamed that God in his mysterious providence would allow this confusion to come about among the four girls, so that the Garabandal event itself would become a prophetic symbol of the latent confusion in the Church that was about to erupt so violently because of the opening of the windows at Vatican II by Pope John XXIII? The staunch opposition of the bishops of Santander to the apparitions and the known openness of Rome on the matter are another facet of this confusion in the Church symbolized by the Garabandal event.

16

Prophecies Awaiting Fulfillment

The most important prophecies made by Our Lady at Garabandal still await fulfillment. These are the warning, the miracle and the permanent sign at the pines, and the chastisement. Enough was said of the miracle in Chapter 1. More needs to be said of the warning and of the chastisement.

The Warning

In addition to the outline of the more important features of the warning given in Chapter 1, we add the following details, all verbatim statements made by Conchita in various letters or in response to questions put to her.

> This warning, like the chastisement, is a very fearful thing for the good as well as the wicked. It will draw the good closer to God and it will warn the wicked that the end of time [not to be confused with the end of the world] is coming and that these are the last warnings. No one can stop it from happening. It is certain, although I know nothing of the day or the date.[1]

[1] From a letter written by Conchita on June 2, 1965, and published in the *Journal de Conchita,* a French annotated translation of *Conchita's Diary* and of certain other documents relating to the Garabandal event. It is the work of G. du Pilier (Paris: Nouvelles Editions Latines, 1967). The letter is found on page 52, note (66).

The warning will be like a revelation of our sins, and it will be seen and experienced equally by believers and non-believers and people of any religion whatsoever. It is like a purification for the miracle. And it is like a catastrophe. It will make us think of the dead, that is, we would prefer to be dead than to experience the warning. The warning will be recognized and accepted by the world as a direct sign from God, and for this reason I believe it is impossible that the world could be so hardened as not to change.[1]

Jesus will send the warning to purify us so that we may better appreciate the miracle by which he clearly proves his love for us and hence his desire that we fulfill the message. It is like a chastisement. We shall see the consequences of the sins we have committed. I think that those who do not despair will experience great good from it for their sanctification.[2]

The warning is something supernatural and will not be explained by science. It will be seen and felt. It will be a correction of the conscience of the world. Those who do not know Christ (non-Christians) will believe it is a warning from God.[3]

Joey Lomangino Will Recover His Sight

A prophecy yet to be fulfilled and which is linked with the prophecy of "the great miracle" concerns "The Blind American," Joey Lomangino of Linden-

[1] Answers to questions submitted to Conchita on September 14, 1965 by Joey Lomangino and several friends.

[2] Taken from a report written by Conchita on December 10, 1965, describing an apparition that had occurred on November 13 of that year. In this report she added the above details concerning the warning, affirming she had received them prior to November 13.

[3] Answers to questions submitted to Conchita in October, 1968, by Mr. and Mrs. Robert Froehlich of New York State.

hurst, Long Island, New York. Our Lady told Conchita in a locution at the pines on March 19, 1964
that Joey would recover his sight on the day of the
great miracle. She said that the first thing he would
see would be the miracle. As Joey has become one
of the greatest apostles of Garabandal in the entire
world today, it is quite obvious that the prophecy
concerning his eyes has more than a strictly personal
connotation. It was Our Lady's way of associating
Joey publicly with the Garabandal event. He is in
reality the fifth person of the Garabandal happenings
and must be ranked along with the four visionaries
as an essential part of these happenings.[1]

The Chastisement

God is just, as well as loving and merciful, a fact that
many have difficulty in accepting today. Because he
is just he punishes. But because he is loving and
merciful, he seeks to bring us back to him through
his punishments. "The Blessed Virgin . . . told me
that Jesus is not going to send the chastisement to
discourage us, but to help us and to reprimand us for
not heeding him," Conchita wrote in the December
10, 1965 report mentioned above. God's seeking to
purify us through the chastisement is also the purpose he pursues through the warning, which Conchita
has described as being "like a chastisement."

God's love and mercy shows itself again in the
chastisement in that it is conditional and announced
well in advance. The chastisement can be averted,
Conchita tells us in her *Diary,* "if the world changes."

The chastisement will apparently be proportioned

---

[1] There will be a considerable section on Joey Lomangino
in *Our Lady Comes to Garabandal.* It will show that he has
a special charisma in regard to the Garabandal event.

to the degree of evil in the world when it occurs. "Just as the chastisement will be very, very great, in keeping with our deserts, so too, the miracle will be extremely great, in keeping with the needs of the world," Conchita tells us in the *Diary*.

Previews of the Chastisement

It is significant that the girls were never given a preview of the miracle but they were shown the chastisement twice during visions. These two ecstasies occurred at night in June, 1962, about a month before the miracle of the visible Host. On the first occasion only Loli and Jacinta were involved. On the second one, Conchita, who had missed the first vision through illness, was with the other two girls. Both nights, shouts of horror came from the frightened children. On the second night, when the cries of terror were even more distressing, some people were able to make out the following words: "Oh! May little children die before this happens! May people have time to go to confession beforehand!"

A Franciscan priest who was preaching in the village was present and asked the spectators to pray. As the prayers began, the cries subsided and the girls seemed to stop suffering. But as soon as the prayers ceased, the cries resumed louder than ever.[1]

As Conchita says in her *Diary:*

And now as we all await this great day of the miracle, let us see if the world changes and the chastisement is averted.

[1] See Father M. Laffineur's book *L'Etoile dans la Montagne* (Bruges, 1966), no. 23, pp. 53-54.

17

To Sum It All Up

God Speaks to Us — The message of Garabandal is the important thing. To capture our attention and galvanize us into saving action, God sent this message through the exciting medium of "apparitions." He sent the Mother of Jesus, as he had sent the prophets of old, to speak in his name.

Leading Good Lives — The message is not new. It is the gospel message applied to our times. Its main theme, which re-echoes the Old and New Testament, is our need for a conversion of heart; we must ask forgiveness for our sins and strive to lead good lives.

Penance and the Passion — The principal means proposed to help us become a holy people are, again, the Old and New Testament means of prayer and penance. Great stress was placed on these. We were told that it was important to make many sacrifices, to perform much penance and to think about the passion of Jesus. Reflection on the passion will inspire us to do penance and make sacrifices.

Prayer and the Rosary — Prayer, a renewed and meaningful prayer, was urged. One prayer, the rosary, was unfailingly recommended every time Our Lady appeared and its recitation was made an integral part of each of her visits.

The Eucharist and the Priest — The Eucharist, the great New Testament means of holiness, figured very prominently in the message. Holy Communion and visiting the Blessed Sacrament were the object of particular attention. The priest, the very special man appointed by God to lead his People to holiness, was also the object of great concern. Though Marian in its context, the main thrust of the Garabandal event is eucharistic and sacerdotal.

Mary Our Mother, the Scapular and "Kissed Objects" — Presiding over the entire event in God's name and fulfilling the motherly function given to her by Jesus at the foot of the cross was Mary. She invited us to wear the brown scapular of Mount Carmel as the symbolic mantle of her protection and she left us "kissed objects" as especially helpful sacramentals, that is, as perpetual reminders of her motherly love and of the power of her intercession with her divine Son. As she told Conchita during her final visit on November 13, 1965: "I have come for all my children so that I may draw them closer to my heart. . . . I hold them all beneath my mantle. . . . I shall always be with you and with all my children."

And Other Things — Obedience to the Church, modesty, belief in the angels and their power to help us and recourse to Saint Michael against the devil, were other things that Our Lady recommended to us at this time of confusion and disbelief in the Church.

Father Joseph A. Pelletier received a Baccalaureate and Licentiate in Sacred Theology from the Pontifical Institute Angelicum (Rome) in 1937. He then returned to his alma mater, Assumption College, Worcester, Massachusetts, where he taught social sciences and religion for ten years. A Master's degree in Sociology was obtained from Boston College in 1947. For the past twenty years he has served on the administrative staff of Assumption College.

His avocation as a writer began with his book *The Sun Danced at Fatima* published in 1951. An immediate success, the book went through five printings (35,000 copies) in a year-and-a-half and was translated into French. It was followed in 1954 by *Fatima Hope of the World*. These books gained for Father Pelletier a world-wide reputation as an authority on Fatima.

Father Pelletier continued his apostolate of the word through frequent lectures and religious articles in American and Canadian Catholic monthlies.

He is now dedicating his pen to the appearances of Our Lady and the other extraordinary phenomena that occurred four-and-a-half year span (June 1961 to February, 1966) Spanish mountain village of San Sebastian de Garaband works on this subject are characterized by the same s approach—painstaking research and scrupulous relia authentic documents—and by the same easy, limpid st marked his books on Fatima and his other writings.

His introductory piece, an illustrated flyer entitled *The* tions of Our Lady at Garabandal, has already been hi claimed. The present pamphlet *Garabandal Prayer* *Rosary* was quickly followed by a first book dealing pr with the message and entitled *God Speaks at Garab* second book *Our Lady Comes to Garabandal*, stres story of the apparitions, is expected to appear late in 19